Alfa Romeo Giulia Spiders and Coupes

Alfa Romeo Giulia Spiders and Coupes

Richard Bremner

MOTOR RACING PUBLICATIONS LTD
Unit 6, The Pilton Estate, 46 Pitlake, Croydon CR0 3RY, England

First published 1992

British Library Cataloguing in Publication Data

Bremner, Richard
   Alfa Romeo Giulia spiders and coupes.
   I. Title
   629.2222

   ISBN 0-947981-59-4

Typeset by Ryburn Publishing Services,
and originated by Ryburn Reprographics, Halifax, West Yorkshire

Printed in Great Britain by
The Amadeus Press Ltd, Huddersfield, West Yorkshire

Contents

Acknowledgements

It was bright red, glistened beneath the raindrops of a recent cloudburst and looked like no coupe I had ever seen. And it was for sale, at just £395. Within minutes I was seduced, broke and the owner of a 1969 1750 GTV. And in one hour I would be stranded, too, steam rising expensively from beneath a bonnet that was soon to become the GTV's most opened panel. This Alfa was one of the worst cars I have ever bought. It rarely went, hated stopping and had more faults than an amateur tennis match. But it had me hooked. I've owned four GTVs now (including the blue 2000 on the cover) along with a Spider, an Alfasud Ti and a 1959 Giulietta Sprint. The disease has struck hard, and writing this book, I'm happy to say, hasn't cured me of it.

Nor, for that matter, has writing about cars for a living (as deputy editor of *CAR Magazine*) which, along with this threateningly expensive addiction to Alfas, I hope qualifies me to write this book. Not that it would have been possible without the help of a large number of people, several of whom I'd like to thank, including Tim Holmes, Neil Warrior and David Thomas of Alfa GB, Rinaldo Hercolani and Neil Verweij of Alfa Romeo at Arese, Mike Buckler and Mike Brown (who between them contributed most of the wisdom contained in Chapter 12), Richard Gadeselli of Fiat, Alec Turnbull, Michael Lindsay of the Alfa Romeo Owners Club, the press offices at ItalDesign and Pininfarina, Mervyn Franklyn, who took the cover photograph and several of the colour shots inside, various photographers of *CAR* and *Supercar Classics* and, above all, Jane Bearman, who suffered the most.

Richard Bremner

CHAPTER 1

Birth of a sensation

'Alfa Romeo is not merely a make of automobile; it is truly something more than a conventionally built car. There are many automotive makes, among which Alfa Romeo stands apart. It is a kind of affliction, an enthusiasm for a means of transport. It is a way of living, a very special way of perceiving the motor vehicle. What it resists is definition. Its elements are like those of the human spirit which cannot be explained in logical terms. They are sensations, passions, things that have much more to do with man's heart than with his brain.'

Thoughts like these probably don't leap to the front of the mind when you shift to fifth at 110mph in a 2000 GTV, or fold the hood of a Spider for a balmy afternoon's cruising. But if you are hooked on Alfas and sometimes wonder why, these words might help. They ought to, because they come from a man who should know – Orazio Satta Puliga, the engineer behind virtually every mass-produced Alfa since the Second World War. It was he who oversaw the birth of the twin-cam four that has been with Alfa since the Fifties, he who conceived the 1900 saloon that took the company into a new age after the war, and he who was responsible for the Giulia Sprint GT and the Spider, ensuring that the Alfa character was successfully preserved in their make-up.

It's a character that stems from a philosophy of advanced engineering – an approach evident even in the earliest Alfas – and the strong belief that what made a race car go well would also help a road car, which is why Alfas tend to have such exciting specifications. Twin overhead camshafts,

hemi-heads, disc brakes all round and five-speed gearboxes are common these days, even in pretty mundane cars, but when the Giulia saloon arrived in 1962 they were rare in cars of any price, let alone in the middle ground that Alfa had taken by then. These are the things that make the Giulia Sprint and the Spider desirable, and of course their styling.

More than 60 years separate the birth of Alfa Romeo and the arrival of these much loved progeny, so perhaps it is naive to think that there can be any link between these cars and the pre-First World War machines beyond four wheels and a piston engine. It's true that the Spider and Sprint have about as much in common with the first Alfas as they do with a Citroen DS or a Datsun Sunny, but perhaps with good reason because the first Alfas weren't Alfas at all, but Darracqs built in Milan under licence from the French company. This was not a bad way for a car company to get started, except that the Darracq was about as suitable for the Italian roads of the time as a roadsweeper is today for the M25 motorway which encircles London.

In fact the company was originally called SAID (Societa Anonima Italiana Darracq) and was set up in 1907 as an outpost of the Darracq company in order to off-load examples of the French company's earlier models on the Italians, who were thought to be pretty ignorant when it came to choosing cars, not least because there were so few of them about and their roads were under-developed. However, this proved to be a serious misjudgment because, even in embryonic form, the Italians' love for the car was deep enough for them to spot a dog when they saw it, and the

7

The original Alfa was merely a French Darracq, built under licence in Italy. It was unsuitable for Italian roads, and virtually killed A. L. F. A. before it was born. This is a 1908 8/10 HP, in obvious need of attention. ALFA ROMEO ARCHIVES

Darracq was certainly that. The upshot was near bankruptcy for SAID in 1910.

But the managing director of the company, Ugo Stella, being convinced that scope for better sales was there if he had the right product, reformed the company and took on a new engineer. Competition on the Italian market was there, but he reckoned there was room for another player besides Fiat (which had 60% of the market even then), Isotta Fraschini and Lancia. The new engineer was Giuseppe Merosi, who successfully designed a new range of cars that would cope with the Italian road conditions.

Merosi was Alfa's first great engineer. The company's history is marked by the reign of three brilliant engineers who were behind every car produced up to the Alfetta of the Seventies.

Merosi was the first, and he was succeeded by Vittorio Jano in 1923, who in turn was replaced by Satta in 1946. But this is leaping ahead somewhat.

The car that got the new firm off the ground was Merosi's 24 HP, which appeared late in 1910 and was the first car to bear the Alfa badge. Stella and his managers felt that it was highly desirable to distance the new range from the SAID-badged Darracqs and so the car was given a new set of initials – ALFA. They stood for Anonima Lombarda Fabbrica Automobili. The Romeo bit would come later.

The 24 HP, a large open tourer powered by a four-cylinder engine of 4.1 litres (the large capacity was a reaction to the puny, under-engined Darracqs), was built on a massive chassis designed to take the beating that the rough Italian roads would undoubtedly give it. Not particularly sporting, the new car nevertheless featured some advanced engineering for its day, amongst which were a block and cylinder-head cast in one and bolted to an alloy crankcase, and the use of a propshaft rather than chain drive.

The car remained fundamentally unaltered for four years, but it was given a power increase in 1914, when it was renamed the 20–30 HP. Around 100 of these cars were stored in component form after the outbreak of the First World War, for later assembly, a move that was to prove fortuitous.

Emboldened by the success of the 24 HP, Alfa expanded its range, first with the smaller 15 HP in 1911 (which became the 15–20 HP when it gained more power in later life) and then in 1913 with its first sports model, the 40–60 HP, a powerful car with a 6–litre four-cylinder engine equipped with overhead valves rather than the

The 1910 24 HP was the first real Alfa, designed by Giuseppe Merosi. A massive car, it was powered by a 4.1-litre four-cylinder engine, the iron block and head of which were cast as one and gave the car a 65mph top speed. Its ladder chassis was exceptionally strong, a reaction to the flimsiness of the Darracq. GRAHAM HARRISON

A 20–30 HP of 1921, this car was a more potent development of the 24 HP, sporting 49bhp rather than 45bhp. Examples of this car were stored in component form during the First World War, for later assembly. ALFA ROMEO ARCHIVES

Alfa's first Grand Prix car used a four-cylinder engine featuring twin cams, four valves per cylinder and twin spark plugs, even in 1914. Despite the technology, it proved underpowered. ALFA ROMEO ARCHIVES

side valves of the lesser models.

Alfa's competition career had begun in 1911 with lighter-weight, cut-down versions of the 24 HP, called the Corsa, but these were still too heavy to pull off any major victories, although they did perform well enough to publicize the Alfa name, which was the main point of the exercise. But the arrival of the 40–60 HP gave Alfa the opportunity to go racing with the prospect of major successes, and several victories were scored with this model during a competition career that was interrupted by the First World

War but was destined to last until 1922.

Despite a distinct shortage of cash, Alfa had decided to enter a car for the new Grand Prix formula which was established in 1914, and because there was no money available to develop a necessary lightweight chassis, the 40–60 HP's standard chassis was shortened while a major effort was applied to developing a more competitive engine to power it.

What emerged was significant for Alfa because the engine featured a sophisticated cylinder-head layout that subsequently was to be found on most of the company's production cars, and is one of the reasons why they have usually offered well above average performance. It included twin camshafts to drive two rows of inclined valves let into the roof of hemispherical combustion chambers, a set-up that ensures excellent gas flow and flame propagation. The 88bhp produced by the 4.5–litre engine was a good result for the day, but it was still not good enough in view of the car's excessive weight and its overly large frontal area, and it was clear that Alfa's first Grand Prix car was unlikely to be a winner. In any case, its chance to compete never arrived because Italy was soon at war and motor racing came to a stop.

By this time the factory had produced almost 1,200 cars in its first five years, but it was in deep financial trouble. Its rescue was to come from one Nicola Romeo, an entrepreneur whose businesses supplying the war effort were expanding so quickly that he badly needed more space, and the ailing Alfa company, in which he had bought a stake, was to provide it. Production of cars stopped, to be replaced by the creation of everything from air compressors to aircraft engines and flamethrowers.

At the war's end, however, the inevitable happened and the factory found itself with a much thinner order book – flamethrowers were not what the war-torn nation most urgently needed. The answer was to drag out the 100

The man who put the Romeo in Alfa, Nicola Romeo bought into the company in 1915 to provide himself with extra capacity to produce war materiel before buying the company outright in 1918. An industrialist with no interest in cars, he was nevertheless largely responsible for Alfa's survival in the tough postwar years. ALFA ROMEO ARCHIVES

The 1923 P2 Grand Prix car, racer Ugo Sivocci at the wheel, shortly before he was killed in it. As a mark of respect the model was never raced again. ALFA ROMEO ARCHIVES

A 1925 RLSS, last of the highly successful six-cylinder RL series that ran from 1922 to 1926, spawning numerous equally successful sports models on the way. GRAHAM HARRISON

models – mostly 20–30s – stored in component form and to assemble them, and these became the first cars to be badged as Alfa Romeos.

In a bid to make the world aware that Alfa was back, competition activities were restarted with the 40–60, the 20–30 and the Grand Prix car, although the latter was to be as unsuccessful as its prewar trials had suggested it would be. But victories were picked up by the two production-based models, and in the meantime Merosi busied himself designing a new car.

After a couple of abortive attempts, known as the G1 and G2, he resorted to a shelved Grand Prix car design that had been experimented with as a potential replacement for the original effort. Although this design was subsequently abandoned because the rules had been changed (there's nothing new, it seems, in the Grand Prix game), it offered promise as the basis for a series of new cars, which were to be known as the RLs.

Though fitted with a new 3-litre six-cylinder engine, the first RL was not particularly fast because it was encumbered with heavy bodywork, wide gear ratios and a low state of tune. But it was reliable, it began to sell, and it proved capable of considerable development through paring weight, shortening the chassis and, above all, raising the power output of the engine. By the end of 1922 more than 800 RLs had been built, and development of the car was still continuing.

The final versions, the RLSS and RLTF (for Super Sport and Targa Florio) were distinctly sporting, the kind of cars people increasingly

associated with Alfa. The TF, as its name suggested, was a race version, and in 1923, when it won the Targa Florio and numerous other races, it did much to ram home the message that Alfa Romeo was a sporting brand. It is this victory in the 1923 Targa Florio which is celebrated by the four-leaf clover emblem which has for so long been associated with Alfas. The victorious car, driven by Ugo Sivocci, wore a pair of quadrifoglio verde on each flank of its bonnet as a good luck charm, and this as been used on every factory racer and many road cars since.

With this kind of success coming their way, it wasn't surprising that the Alfa management began to think again about an onslaught on the Grand Prix Championship, so Merosi was commissioned once again to build a car. This time he had the proverbial blank pad in front of him, and he produced a twin-carburettor 2-litre six-cylinder engine, again with twin cams, inclined valves and hemispherical combustion chambers, and mounted it in a chassis considerably shorter than the RL's. A twin-spark ignition system was also featured, a solution which would be seen again in the Sprint GT-based GTA Alfa raced in the Sixties.

The P1, as it became known, had close-fitting, streamlined bodywork made from aluminium to save weight (again an approach used for the GTA), but rather poor roadholding which, sadly, was to kill Sivocci during a test session at Monza on the eve of the 1923 Italian Grand Prix. The car never raced again.

Although Nicola Romeo didn't give up on his

The car that won Alfa its first Grand Prix World Championship in 1925, the P2, was the creation of Vittorio Jano, one of the great Alfa designers. The P2 used a twin-cam, supercharged straight-eight that produced as much as 175bhp for a 140mph top speed. Alfa's championship victory was celebrated with the addition of a wreath to the badge, a detail that survived until relatively recently. ALFA ROMEO ARCHIVES

Grand Prix dreams, he also needed new cars to sell. The RL and its smaller sister, the four-cylinder RM, had done well, but they were becoming dated and needed successors. Romeo was also in need of a new chief engineer because Merosi had left the company.

The man who replaced him was Vittorio Jano, who was head-hunted from the Fiat racing team on behalf of Alfa by his friends Luigi Bazzi and Enzo Ferrari. At this time Ferrari was one of Alfa's works drivers, and he would eventually manage Alfa's racing effort before setting up his own company. In the meantime he acted as a go-between in the negotiations that finally resulted in Jano moving from Fiat into the Alfa camp.

Jano rapidly produced a new Grand Prix car, the P2. Although it retained some of the P1's features, such as a ladder-frame chassis and a twin-cam engine, it differed in a number of crucial respects. It was smaller, lighter, and had a reduced frontal area, improving its aerodynamics. There were also differences in suspension design, but the most important changes concerned the power unit, which this time was a straight-eight, and supercharged. The P2 also had good looks on its side, both in style and detail, and there was an aggressive simplicity in its shape, as well as one of the most stunning exhaust manifolds you could hope to see.

It was design of this quality that led many to compare Jano's work with that of the Bugattis and with great artists in other fields. Nor did such esteem prove to be misplaced because the P2 won first time out, and the following year, 1925, it

brought Alfa Romeo its first World Championship, in celebration of which an encircling garland was added to the badge.

But it was not just Jano's design skills that gave him greatness, it was also his vision. In the mid-Twenties Alfa rather unwisely concentrated on racing at the expense of getting on with its road car programme, which led to the creation of much pent-up demand for its cars, but no modern design with which to satisfy it. Profits were not coming the firm's way, but Jano managed to rescue matters by turning the P2 into a road car. He removed the supercharger and sliced off two cylinders to create the 6C 1500. The new car was smaller and lighter than the RL, and its engine was also smaller, but because it was more efficient it performed just as well. For various reasons, production of this car was delayed for two years after it had first been shown in 1925, but once assembly got underway further models were developed to supplement the modestly powered original version, the engine of which, despite its GP origins, produced only 44bhp. First came a Sport version, and this was followed by a short-wheelbase Super Sport model which, when optionally ordered with a supercharger, was good for 76bhp and 87mph.

Although Alfa Romeo was now out of Grand Prix racing, it decided to re-enter production racing events, and in 1927 it won the first Mille Miglia with a 6C 1500. Soon after this, one of the most famous of all prewar Alfas was to emerge as a development of the 1500 – the 6C 1750, part of whose name was to get a reprise in the Sixties on

Cutting two cylinders from the P2's straight eight and installing it in a compact chassis produced the 6C 1500s, this pretty short-wheelbase SS Mille Miglia model dating from 1928. This version had a twin-cam head and a supercharger, and produced 76bhp. ALFA ROMEO ARCHIVES

A Zagato-bodied 1750 Gran Sport, one of the most famous and beautiful of all prewar Alfas. The series was built between 1929 and 1933 and was the car after which the 1750 Spider, GTV and Berlina of 1969 were named. This car's twin-cam 1,752cc supercharged six-cylinder engine, developed from the 1500, produced 85bhp at 4,500rpm. ALFA ROMEO ARCHIVES

The 6C 2300 was a development of the original 1750s and 1900s, and did much to revive Alfa's wilting sales after it was introduced in 1934. This beautiful open version is another of the more famous prewar cars, though the less exciting saloons formed the bulk of sales. ALFA ROMEO ARCHIVES

the bootlids of Spiders and Sprints.

Like the 6C 1500 and RLs before it, the 1750 began life in modest tune, but it was not long before more exotic twin-cam, lightweight and supercharged versions developed, producing further victories for Alfa in the Mille Miglia and Targa Florio. The ultimate version of the 1750, a supercharged, 85bhp,, 90mph, open-top sportscar known as the Gran Sport, was also produced as a closed car and dubbed the Gran Turismo. And so the first GT car was born.

The 6C 1500 and the 6C 1750 were the most popular Alfas yet, 596 of the first series and 2,776 of the second series being sold. Jano followed these designs with the more flamboyant 8C 2300 in 1931, whose straight-eight engine was unusual in being made up of two fours in series. These were derived from the Grand Prix P2's engine, which he cut in half, turning each half through 180 degrees and mounting the cam drives and auxiliaries between them, the object being to reduce the length of the cams and crankshaft, so lessening whip and improving reliability.

The 8C 2300s were fine examples of engineering and great to drive, but they presented further evidence that Alfa often failed to distinguish the difference between cars the public

desired and cars they could actually afford. This was an expensive prestige car that cost double the price of the old 1750, and it was launched in the aftermath of the Wall Street crash. The 2300 may have won races, but it certainly wasn't winning Alfa sales, and by 1933 production was less than half what it had been four years earlier.

Dwindling profits began to hit the company hard, in fact it was so short of cash that it had to withdraw its Grand Prix team, whose latest machine, the 2.7-litre, 215bhp P3, had proven highly successful during 1932, its debut year, carrying off so much silverware that Alfa seemed certain of further major success the following year. But the money simply wasn't there to chase yet more trophies. In fact, it wasn't there to pursue any activity at all, let alone one as profligate as racing, until, that is, the government stepped in, in the name of the newly constituted IRI (Istituto Ricostruzione Industriale), an outfit formed to keep shaky Italian businesses shored up and reduce unemployment. The government already owned some shares in Alfa Romeo, and this solution effectively acquired it the rest.

Alfa would survive, and its activities would increasingly turn towards the manufacture of aircraft engines and trucks to support Benito

Mussolini's armaments programme. But it would also support his efforts to garner Italy prestige by going racing again. The P3s were dragged out of storage and took to the tracks once more.

What was needed more than all this, however, was a new car to sell, and this Jano swiftly created. He took the old 1750 six-cylinder engine, which had already been converted into a 1900 in its most recent versions, and expanded it again to 2.3 litres. This engine was mounted in a new chassis of pressed steel rather than girders, which helped to keep the price to less than half that of the 8C 2300. The result was not a desperately exciting beast, but within a year this formula had sold more examples than the 8C had managed over the previous four years. And despite Alfa's severe financial troubles, its management couldn't resist making a sportscar out of their new design, creating more potent short-wheelbase versions, three examples of which were entered in a 24-hour race held at Pescara. The trio came home first, second and third, scoring a victory which led to a series of sports and touring cars being called the Pescara.

The story of Alfa's remaining years to the Second World War is one in which ever less attention was paid to production machinery and ever more to the company's – and the nation's – efforts in the Grand Prix world. This had become the stage for national muscle-flexing, and no country strutted with quite the confidence of Germany, which fielded immensely successful teams from Mercedes-Benz and Auto Union. Money was not a consideration in this competition, and the championship contest became a relentless race for ever more horsepower and was invariably won by the Germans.

That didn't stop the Italians from trying, however, and Jano set about producing ever more powerful machinery to take on the Germans. Few of these attempts were successful, but some of the cars were fascinating, none more so than the awesome Bimotore, which had a P3 engine mounted at each end to drive all four wheels. It produced more than 500bhp, offered spectacular acceleration and could top 200mph, but its frequent visits to the pits for more tyres rather undermined its speed advantage.

Repeated lack of success in the Grand Prix world led to a diversion and the arrival of a highly successful sportscar in the 8C 2900A, which used the chassis of one of the Grand Prix cars powered

The P3 Grand Prix racer scored some early success, but became a victim of Alfa's dire financial condition, the racing team being folded up while at the height of competitiveness. After a six-month interlude in which the Italian government stepped in to bail Alfa out, the P3s returned to find a Grand Prix world that had moved on and victories that were harder to come by. ALFA ROMEO ARCHIVES

This fabulously expensive 2900B 8C, its bodywork fabricated by coachbuilders Touring, would be one of Alfa's last prewar cars, sold to a dwindling market about to be obliterated by the Second Word War. It was powered by a 180bhp supercharged straight-eight engine. Only 30 2900Bs were built. ALFA ROMEO ARCHIVES

by a stretched version of the old straight-eight, a combination good enough to bring a one-two-three result in the 1936 Mille Miglia and victory in the Spa 24-hours race.

Meanwhile, Jano made his final attempt at a winning Grand Prix car, producing a 4.5-litre V12 capable of 190mph. But it broke its rear axle at the 1937 Italian Grand Prix and that finally broke Jano's resolve. He resigned, defeated. Alfa made one more attempt on the title before the war without him, producing a car powered by a massive and complex V16 engine, which turned out to be almost as unsuccessful. But some good did come out of it because a bank of the engine was taken to produce a 1.5-litre straight-eight for use in a car complying with a new voiturette formula conceived for races in support of the Grands Prix. This compact, pretty machine was called the Alfetta; it won many of the supporting races, but more important, it was to gain Alfa Romeo many victories when Grand Prix racing resumed after the war, including the first two postwar World Championships in 1950 and 1951.

Alfa's production car activities in the late Thirties were to prove irrelevant to the needs of a struggling postwar world. Since it was not essential to turn a profit, the company concentrated on selling increasingly luxurious and potent sports models. The stopgap 2300 model that saved the company in the early Thirties was stretched to 2.5 litres to produce cars that were sporting and luxurious rather than mass-market machines, the upshot being that less than 100 of them were made. But these cars were commonplace compared with the magnificent race car-based 2900B, of which only 30 appeared in long or short-wheelbase forms. These were marvellous cars, but as Alfa was to find out six years later, not what the market needed in 1945. In the short term, Alfa was going to have plenty to do during the Second World War, but afterwards it was not going to be able to make a living out of toys for bloated plutocrats. In a very different postwar world, a revolution of sorts would be needed.

CHAPTER 2

Postwar jewels

The Second World War hit Alfa Romeo hard, literally. Its factory at Portello had been bombed, almost a third of its machinery had been destroyed, and the sales network had disappeared completely. On top of that, over the previous 10 years the plant had been geared up for the production not of cars, but of aircraft engines and assorted war materiel.

These were setbacks guaranteed to keep the management awake at night, especially as the factory was forbidden from making the things it had been turning out during the war. Something new had to be produced. There was considerable pressure to continue manufacturing because the Milanese factory now had an idle workforce of thousands, the numbers having been swollen by the demands of war. These were men and women who desperately needed to keep their jobs, and if

that meant working in buildings that had no heaters and no glass in their windows they weren't going to complain too loudly.

Production of cars was virtually impossible to start with, so Alfa concentrated instead on some surprising sidelines, producing such things as roller shutters, window frames and domestic cookers (which flaunt marvellously bold Alfa Romeo script on their oven doors) while simultaneously rebuilding the damaged factory. By the end of the first year 80% of the plant was operational again, over 1,100 machine tools were in working order, and effort was gradually being directed at doing what the factory knew best – making cars.

In 1945 it managed to turn out just three 6C 2500s, cars part-assembled from components salted away during the war, and the following year

Stocks of parts stored before the war provided the basis of this special-bodied 6C 2500. Though Alfa sold nearly 700 cars using these mechanicals after the War, the majority of them coach-built, they were not really appropriate for a market that needed something cheaper.
ALFA ROMEO ARCHIVES

17

Alfa Romeo's first all-new postwar design, the 1900 saloon, proved a commercial success with over 7,600 sold between 1950 and 1953. It looked as unexciting as any Fiat or Ford, but beneath the surface sat surprisingly sporting mechanicals. This was the first Alfa Romeo to come with left-hand drive, right-hand drive being favoured previously to aid seeing the verge at night. ALFA ROMEO ARCHIVES

the number rose to over 160. But it wasn't until 1947 that something fresh emerged from Portello, though it was hardly radical. The Freccia D'Oro (Golden Arrow) was a rebodied 6C 2500, available either as an Alfa-bodied saloon, a sports tourer by Pininfarina, or a coupe by Touring. There were a few mechanical modifications, but they ran to no more than a column gearchange instead of a floor shift and re-rated shock absorbers. However, the biggest difference – that the body was welded to the separate chassis – was significant as a prelude to the arrival of the monocoque 1900 saloon.

Despite its relatively exclusive nature, the Freccia D'Oro sold well, almost 2,000 finding buyers in the four years from 1947 to 1951, among whom were Prince Rainier of Monaco, King Farouk of Egypt and the actress Rita Hayworth. But this was not the car to keep Alfa in business. Its mechanicals were essentially prewar and its appeal too exclusive to keep a factory and workforce of Portello's size busy and profitable. Something genuinely fresh was needed.

It came from the young Orazio Satta Puliga, the third of Alfa's great engineers, and it was called the 1900. Viewed today, this somewhat plump saloon looks about as sporty as a Morris Oxford,

only its interesting grille saving it from total anonymity. But although the 1900 was a relatively prosaic design, its arrival was a watershed for Alfa. Here was a modern concept and the kind of car the market actually wanted, a subtlety Alfa had previously missed with appalling regularity.

The 1900 is also important to our story because encased within it were a series of engineering solutions that anyone who owns a Giulia will find familiar. There was the monocoque body, of course, but the running gear was at least as significant because its format would reign until the early Seventies and the arrival of the Alfetta and the Alfasud.

Though superficially simple, consisting of an in-line engine mounted up front, the transmission behind it driving a propshaft that turned a live axle, there were subtleties in the design that made it stand out. The live axle, for example, was coil rather than leaf-sprung, the dampers being mounted within the coils, and it was located by trailing arms and an ingenious pair of rods that triangulated the top of the diff to the body. They improved location and reduced unsprung weight because the axle was now part-hung directly from the shell. The front suspension was more

18

conventional, consisting of coil springs and double wishbones, but it was certainly one of the soundest solutions. But what really saved this saloon from total obscurity was its engine.

Those who feared that Alfa's prewar engineering traditions had been completely abandoned were reassured after a glance under the 1900's domed bonnet, where the alloy covers of a twin-cam engine were on display. True, it was a four-cylinder of modest capacity, but it used an alloy cylinder-head, centrally placed spark plugs and the inclined valves that so many of its ancestors had featured. It was far from unsporting, allowing the 1900 a top speed of 90mph, the speed of Morris Oxford drivers' dreams.

The choice of four cylinders was not an easy one for Satta. This was a car that was meant to take Alfa downmarket to a wider audience, but he didn't want to risk squandering the company's reputation for quality engineering by building a car that could have come from Fiat or Ford. So a six-cylinder version had been in the offing for a while, but then some market research revealed that four pots were what the public really wanted. In any case, one of the main objectives for the 1900 was to make it as light as possible, and deleting a couple of cylinders would certainly help in that direction.

Satta was well placed when it came to extracting performance from the engine because this cylinder-head design generated good combustion characteristics. But there was more to obtaining horsepower than this. In order to run hard the four had to run fast, at crank speeds that would have had prewar engines bursting at the seams. Shortening the stroke and increasing the cylinder bore was the answer so as to reduce the piston velocity for a given crank speed. This had a couple of implications; the combustion chambers would be larger, demanding a greater gas flow for every cycle, which in turn would throw out more heat, but on the other hand they

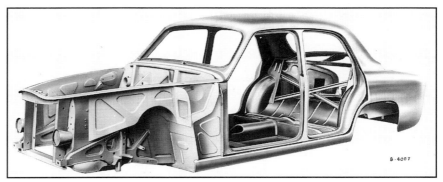

For Alfa, the most radical aspect of the 1900 was the use of monocoque body construction rather than a separate chassis, advantages of which included increased assembly accuracy and lighter weight. The style may be different, but the structure of this shell is very similar to that of a four-door saloon car today. ALFA ROMEO ARCHIVES

Not the sight you'd expect to find under the lid of so prosaic a car, the 1900 used a new 1,975cc twin-cam engine that remained true to Alfa tradition. The engine layout would form the basis of the motor that appeared in the Giuliettas and Giulias and lives on today, in spirit at least, in the Alfa 155. ALFA ROMEO ARCHIVES

This Giulietta Sprint, which began the Alfa tradition for compact coupes, proved to be one of the prettiest designs of the Fifties and led the company further down the mass-production road. Its bodywork was designed by Bertone's Franco Scaglione; the coachbuilder also manufactured, painted and trimmed the bodyshells for Alfa. This is one of the very earliest examples from 1954 and is identifiable by its hatchback, an arrangement shortly to be ditched in favour of a conventional bootlid. ALFA ROMEO ARCHIVES

would allow room for larger valves, which would promote freer breathing.

Alfa's aero engine experience provided a solution to the heat problem, which threatened the exhaust valves. The valve seats were finished in hard-wearing stellite, and the valves themselves were sodium-filled for swifter heat dissipation. The valve stems were chrome-plated for longevity, as were the piston's scraper rings – another aero engineering trick.

The detail of this engine is relevant because its layout and features formed the basis of the power unit which one day would propel the Giulia GT and Spider. Apart from its larger capacity, the 1900's engine differed only in that it used an iron block and a steel sump. It was early proof of the excellence of Satta's work.

The 1900 sold slowly at first because Alfa only made it slowly, but as production increased so did sales, which soon encouraged the introduction of more derivatives. First into the showrooms was

the 1900 TI (after the racing class Turismo Internazionale), which arrived in 1951, a year after the 1900's debut. Larger valves, a higher compression ratio and a twin-choke carburettor pushed its power output up to 100bhp and its top speed to 106mph. Later, the capacity would be increased from 1,884cc to 1,975cc and the 1900s gained a Super prefix to advertise the fact. The company also sold the 1900 chassis to coachbuilders, who occasionally shrouded them in more stunning bodywork. Although these cars didn't sell in volume, they reinforced the message that Alfa Romeo had not forgotten about sportscars. But the real proof of this would come in 1954, when the company introduced the brilliant Giulietta, which it brought to the market in a breathtakingly audacious style.

Alfa's problem was money, a not unfamiliar difficulty at Portello, and in particular raising enough of it to get a new range underway. Though the 1900 had taken the company further

A Sprint from the first series, known as the 750, most obviously identifiable by its slotted side grilles and the absence of any side repeaters. It wasn't just the body that looked good to enthusiasts, who were also given an all-alloy, twin-cam five-bearing engine, forged double-wishbone suspension, ZF worm-and-roller steering, a very well located live rear axle with a lightweight alloy diff casing and wonderful-looking finned brake drums. ALFA ROMEO ARCHIVES

A 750-series Sprint interior, of high quality despite the fact that, in Italy, this was a relatively cheap car. Note the cloth-trimmed seats – eventually to be supplanted by what at that time was trendier vinyl – the two-tone door trims and bound carpets. This car also had an optional radio. The gear-lever was column-mounted for this early series. ALFA ROMEO ARCHIVES

downmarket than before, it hadn't descended sufficiently far to achieve really high-volume sales. The postwar era was not an affluent one, and the market for cars like the 1900 was still relatively small, especially abroad. On top of this, governments, particularly the Italian one, were tending to penalize big-engined cars.

In response to this, the engineers produced what was essentially a miniaturized 1900, although it was not the saloon version of the Giulietta that appeared first, but the Sprint coupe. It turned up late, at the Turin show in April 1954, but it arrived just in time to avoid plunging Alfa Romeo into a national scandal revolving around the methods it had used to raise capital for the Giulietta project.

This involved issuing security bonds yielding interest at six-monthly intervals, but the real come-on was that 200 of the debenture holders would win a Giulietta saloon as a prize for their support. The car was originally to be shown at the Brussels show in late 1953, but it failed to appear there, or at the Geneva show in spring 1954, by which time doubts, and a scandal, were brewing.

The 200 winners had been named, but there were no cars to give to them. Nor was there any prospect of providing them with their prizes in the immediate future because the new body plant was at least a year away from becoming operational. However, the mechanicals for the new car were being produced in low volume, which gave the Giulietta's creators an idea.

With the help of an outside coachbuilder they

could get a limited-edition sports coupe into production, using the new mechanicals, display it at the 1954 Turin show and thereby placate both the 200 winners and the press, who by now were worryingly interested in the affair. The chosen coachbuilder would complete between 500 and 1,000 coupes to supply the winners as well as other enthusiasts, an additional benefit being that having several hundred Giulietta coupes rushing around Italy would build interest in the upcoming saloon, which was a far more important car commercially.

Alfa's task was made considerably easier by the fact that the Giulietta prototype (it was known as a muletto) actually resembled a coupe, and a not unattractive one at that. So this was used as a basis; Nuccio Bertone and Boano of Carrozzeria Ghia were each shown it and given a plaster cast of it, and told to come back with proposals for a production version in 10 days.

It was Bertone's solution that was given the nod, though Boano would help to build the cars because Ghia's facilities were considerably better developed than Bertone's. That, at least, was the theory, until Boano and his employer had a row that led to him walking out and Alfa handing the entire job to Bertone. It was this commission which put Nuccio Bertone on the map, rapidly turning a minor coachbuilder into a major force in the car design business.

The first car was finished with just 20 days to spare before the Turin show, and it was beautiful. Compact, graceful and spared the heavy-handed chrome-plating that disfigured so many designs of the day, it was liked instantly. Alfa had just escaped a major embarrassment.

However, only 12 cars got past the factory gates in 1954, but 1,415 were made the following year and output was up to 3,600 by 1959. At last Alfa Romeo was turning into a volume maker, not that the coupe was the volume seller. That was the role of the saloon, which was launched at the beginning of 1955. It sat on a wheelbase 10in shorter than the 1900's and it had a narrower track, too, changes which helped towards a 440lb weight saving over the 1900 so that it scaled just under 2,000lb. It was not just the smaller body that pared poundage, though – changes to the engine also contributed, not least because the iron block was discarded in favour of an alloy item. There was also a capacity reduction, taking the twin-cam down from the 1,975cc of the later 1900s to just 1,290cc.

The basic design of the engine remained the same, but the valve inclination was reduced from 90 to 80 degrees and the combustion chambers were reshaped for more efficient combustion, allowing a compression ratio of 7.5:1. There was only a single-choke carburettor, which meant a power output of 53bhp which, though not a lot, was sufficient to push a Giulietta saloon to 87mph.

The Sprint, of course, was quicker. Lighter by 77lb, it had a significantly more potent engine with a compression ratio of 8:1, a twin-choke carburettor and an output of 65bhp, which enabled it to reach 98mph, quite an achievement in 1954 for a car with an engine of this capacity. There are plenty of 1.3-litre cars around today that will not match that.

The Sprint was about more that just 'go',

The Giulietta saloon, launched in 1955, was the big-selling model in the range despite Alfa's sporting reputation. It was meant to have been launched before the Sprint, but was delayed by the late arrival of body tooling. It lacked the style of its Sprint and Spider brothers, but went pretty well using much the same running gear. ALFA ROMEO ARCHIVES

Enthusiasts soon discovered the competition potential of the Giuliettas, the Sprints making good weekend racers despite the fact that they roll a lot, as this shot proves. In time, Alfa's competition success would be won with the Sprint-based, Zagato-designed SZ, and then the specialized TZ. ALFA ROMEO OWNERS CLUB

A rare Giulietta Sprint Veloce, identifiable by the sliding Perspex door windows. Later Veloces had conventional glass. ALFA ROMEO OWNERS CLUB

however, because like the saloon it had well-developed suspension. Once again there was a live rear axle located by trailing arms and sprung by coil springs within which the shock absorbers were mounted. But this time Alfa had refined the axle location system, ditching the triangulating rods linking the differential to the underpan in favour of a more substantial A-frame that kept the axle under tighter rein. The steering was by worm and roller and the brakes were inside four enormous alloy drums whose helical cooling fins were an absolute delight to look at.

The early Sprint prototypes were hatchbacks, featuring a lift-up rear door, but the production models, which shared exactly the same shape, had a conventional boot. Though roomy in the front, the Sprint was bad news for those banished to the rear, who sat on pairs of optional clip-in cushions – in the standard cars the rear cabin area was left as a flat tray to which extra luggage could be strapped.

But what mattered more than practicalities like this was that the Sprint was a great drive. That the driver had been given priority over the passengers was confirmed by the fact that the engine was canted to the right to provide him with more leg space, and the fresh-air pipework was ducted in his favour as well, not that one needed to unearth subtleties like these to realize

An early 1954 Giulietta Spider, which was styled and built by Pininfarina. Though it remained essentially the same during its 12-year life, there were numerous detail changes to the design, the most significant of which was a stretch in wheelbase.   ALFA ROMEO ARCHIVES

A later Spider, circa 1956, though still a 750-series. The 750 designation is thought to stem from Alfa's first thoughts for the twin-cam four, which was originally built as a 750cc engine. The front overriders of this car were less bullet-like than for the earliest models, the thin slat bisecting the side grille was chromed and the seat trim was piped.   ALFA ROMEO ARCHIVES

that this was a driver's car.

For a start, the controls were all carefully placed for easy access, and they worked with a silken precision that would have been utterly alien to the owners of the more mundane machinery of the day. Visibility was excellent because the pillars were so slender, and the driver's seat was fairly intelligently upholstered, for the era at least. Instruments were plentiful and included a rev-counter and gauges for oil pressure and temperature, which were still rare on sportscars costing far more.

The promise of all this kit was soon confirmed on the road. The baby twin-cam four would pull with vigour, especially if it was revved hard, never sounding as stressed as rival fours, and it span with real smoothness. Proof lay in the 7,000rpm figures that racers and testers regularly used without bringing on a pocket-savaging repair bill.

Those watching Sprints in action might easily end up believing that they didn't handle too well. Giuliettas always rolled a lot, giving the impression of being on the brink of departing the scene unconventionally. But that was not how it felt in the cockpit. Yes, the Giulietta rolled, but that was the corollary of avoiding a rock-hard ride. The basic handling and grip were fine. The steering was sensitive, and the understeer that grew in tight turns disappeared through speedily taken sweepers, replaced by near-neutrality and a

Giulietta Spiders were given a floor-mounted gearchange virtually from the start, whereas the Sprint and saloon had a column change. Though it looks Spartan today, this was a well-equipped cabin for a cheap roadster, which included wind-up windows, a decent hood, full instrumentation and a lockable glovebox as standard. This is a later, post-1959 Spider on the longer wheelbase, a version identifiable by its quarter-lights. ALFA ROMEO ARCHIVES

great feeling of stability. And the car stopped well, too, unlike some contemporary sportscars.

It is not hard to imagine the demand there might have been for a car that did all this and came with a soft top in place of a steel roof, and that car arrived on October 1, 1955. A two-seat sportscar bodied by Pininfarina, it shared none of the body panels, nor even the wheelbase of its sister saloon and coupe. But it did use the same mechanicals, and since it was lighter it accelerated slightly more briskly, although its 98mph top speed was the same as the Sprint's. There was one small but significant mechanical difference between Spider and Sprint, however, which was the roadster's floor-mounted gearchange, an essential the coupe would have to wait for.

The Spider was a pretty car, and it featured some civilizing equipment that certainly wasn't standard fare with its (mostly British) rivals, including an easily folded and erected hood, wind-up side windows and a decent-sized boot. Despite the absence of a roof to strengthen the shell it handled at least as well as the Sprint, not least because its fractionally shorter wheelbase helped its agility. And scuttle shake, the bane of so many open-top cars, was fairly well contained.

Alfa's production and exports, particularly to the USA, took off, the Giulietta eventually selling 177,688 examples in its 10-year life. This represented a massive expansion for Alfa Romeo which, until the Giulietta arrived, had produced just 33,500 cars in its life that far. As one might expect of a successful product, the Giulietta was regularly upgraded. The most important of these changes occurred towards the end of the Fifties when there was a whole batch of mechanical modifications, seemingly introduced piecemeal, making it impossible to identify a precise date for the various changes. But at an apparently arbitrary point, the factory's identification number for the series changed from the original 750 to 101. The later cars were built using more modern mechanized techniques (which make them a less romantic buy for the purist collector) and the Spider sat on a wheelbase 2in longer, which many felt spoiled its looks, but the modifications to the running gear were worth having because they improved the previously questionable durability of the engine, gearbox and assorted sundries. The range was also enlarged.

A hot saloon, the TI, was to prove the biggest seller of all, but more desirable models today are the Sprint and Spider Veloce, whose twin Weber carburettors boosted power to 90bhp, top speed to 112mph, and chopped the 0–60mph time to around 11sec.

Most desirable of all were the special-bodied Giuliettas. The SS and the SZ were sensational-

Giorgetto Giugiaro facelifted the Sprint subtly and sympathetically, the most obvious change being to the side grilles, which were meshed to match the central shield, making this car a 101-series. Though the car looked much the same, it incorporated significant mechanical improvements, mostly connected with enlarging the bearings of the previously somewhat fragile engine. The gearbox was beefed up, too. This Giulia 1300 Sprint is a late one, built for a short while when the model was reintroduced after the launch of the Giulia Sprint GT, sales of which had started slowly. ALFA ROMEO ARCHIVES

The Giulietta Spider became the Giulia Spider in 1962, when it gained many of the new Giulia Sprint GT's mechanicals as options, including a 1600 engine, disc brakes, stronger suspension and a five-speed gearbox. The Giulias were primarily identifiable by the air intake on the bonnet, necessitated by the taller block of the longer-stroke 1600 engine. ALFA ROMEO ARCHIVES

looking cars whose aerodynamics and lightweight shells made them at least as dramatic and entertaining as Alfa's best prewar cars. Since some of them lived on in Giulia guise as sisters to the Sprint and Spider, they are discussed later.

These were cars that continued a tradition that had won Alfa Romeo worldwide admiration, and from luminaries as bright as Henry Ford, who commented that 'every time an Alfa Romeo goes by I raise my hat'. If this was true, he would have

had a severely aching arm once the Giulietta had started to sell. These were truly successful cars, not just by Alfa Romeo's standards, but internationally. They had taken the firm into profit and driven its name into the consciousness of thousands more people, people who now could actually afford an Alfa. Moreover, this had been done without damaging the company's reputation for building classy, stylish, drivers' cars. Repeating such a feat would not be easy.

CHAPTER 3

Magic box

The car that came next was as ordinary-looking as its predecessor. The first Giulia was a simple-looking saloon, one of the most literal interpretations of the three-box shape there has ever been. At first glance you would think it was designed by a man more used to fashioning cornflakes cartons than cars. But this creation was the first in a series – the 105 models – that would turn out to be the most successful that Alfa has ever produced. The saloon would shortly spawn the coupe and the spider of this book as well as a supercar (the Montreal), various spectacular low-volume specials and some of the most successful racers of the Sixties.

The designer behind it was chief engineer Satta, who had some singular thoughts about the way this car should be. In fact, he had them a long time before work on this project began. In the mid-Fifties, Alfa did some work on a small front-drive car, known as the Tipo 103, which had a transverse 895cc twin-cam engine and front drive. Had this car found company favour, it might well have beaten BMC's Mini to the goal of being the first mass-market, transverse, FWD car. Cash shortages and other priorities got in the 103's way, however, and it was aborted. But its basic style, that simple three-box shape, was to live on in the Giulia saloon.

The engineers at Alfa, and Satta in particular, believed that style was not important for a saloon that was meant to do a straightforward trans-portation job, even if it performed the task with more grace and driver involvement than most. So the coachbuilders and stylists were not very deeply involved.

The aerodynamicists were, though. The most remarkable thing about the Giulia saloon is its drag factor, which seems totally at odds with its blunt shape. Alfa had learnt much about aerodynamics, first with the bizarre-looking BAT cars and later with the beautiful Bertone-built Giulietta SS and Zagato's SZ, and the experience was to pay off in the Giulia saloon. It had a Cd of only 0.34, the same as a Ford Sierra's, one of the most obviously aerodynamic saloons of the Eighties.

The feat was accomplished by concentrating on areas of the body that are critical in ensuring a fluent passage through the air. The cubist Giulia saloon proves conclusively what car designers seem to be learning all over again – that the minutiae are more important than a fundamentally slippery shape. Ask contemporary designers to point out some of the critical, drag-inducing areas, and they will wave a hand at a car's nose, its screen pillars and its rump. And this was where the key to the Giulia's wind-slipping shape lay. It had a short, subtly sloped bonnet – that may seem nothing now, but this was innovation in 1962 – its front windscreen was wrapped around considerably at the sides, directing air more tidily along the car's flanks, and an abrupt Kamm tail with a vertical, recessed rear panel ensured that the body left minimal eddies in its wake.

The boxy shape meant plenty of space for luggage and people, though not the six boldly implied by the bench front seat and column gearchange. But the Giulia was a lot more spacious than the Giulietta saloon, which might well have failed had it not been built in a country where anyone topping 6ft is probably foreign.

The Giulia provided more room because it was

The Giulia TI, launched in 1962, was a boxy but functional beast, but the combination of a 1,570cc twin-cam engine, five-speed transmission and remarkable aerodynamic qualities – it was as slippery as a Ford Sierra – made for a true sports saloon. The mechanicals of this car provided the basis for the Giulia GT and the Spider Duetto. CAR MAGAZINE

The styling of the Tipo 103, an aborted project for a compact front-drive saloon, was the inspiration for the later Giulia saloon, and possibly for the rear-engined Renault R8, too, Alfa having a tie with La Regie at the time that Dauphines and R4s were produced at Arese. Intriguingly, the 103 used an 895cc version of the twin-cam turned sideways to drive the front wheels; had the car made production, it would have been a contemporary of the transverse-engined Mini. This, the sole example built, resides in the Alfa museum. GRAHAM HARRISON

bigger, which was why the tail end of the Giulietta name was lopped off to create the Giulia. The new car sat on a wheelbase 4.8in longer than the old one's, at 98.8in, and it was 6in longer overall. It was broader, too, but not as tall, which made it look sportier, though the main contribution to this aspect was its grille and the four headlamps set within it. The slightly aggressive visage wasn't inappropriate, though, because the Giulia had a larger 1,570cc version of the twin-cam engine.

The extra capacity was found by manufacturing a deeper block, allowing a longer stroke, and by fitting bigger-bore cylinder liners. The valves were larger, too, but the 80-degree angle between them and the basic combustion chamber design remained unchanged. Two of the engineers' goals for the new motor were improved flexibility and greater torque. The capacity increase obviously helped, but so did the choice of carburettor, which was now a dual-choke Solex. Other modifications included making the exhaust manifold in two parts because the single castings had an apparently incurable habit of cracking, and improvements to the cooling system, which was famous for getting hot and bothered in the Giulietta. The new sump, now shaped like a hammer head to clear the front crossmember, was of finned alloy, which must have helped in this direction.

The twin-cam was now becoming a very attractive unit, not just on paper, but also out of a car and on view. It was composed almost entirely from alloy now that the sump was aluminium-based, and must have looked magnificent compared to some of the all-iron pushrod lumps that powered most European cars at the start of the Sixties.

What made the mechanicals still more attractive was the mating of the 1600 with a five-speed gearbox, a sophistication that very few cars offered then, and certainly not in the Giulia's class, and a differential whose housing was now made from alloy to reduce unsprung weight. Not many cars offered suspension as well developed as the new Alfa's, either. Although the format was much the same as the Giulietta's, there were quite a few alterations to upgrade it, not least of which was longer wheel travel, essential if the ride was to improve without undermining the car's agility.

Up front, double wishbones were retained, as was the anti-roll bar, but the dampers were no longer mounted within the coils, and the wishbones themselves were all new. Most importantly, the upper one, now wider-based for superior wheel control, was split in half, the forward arm being adjustable to ease alteration of the castor angle. The rear arm was a simple but substantial transverse link. The wishbones were bolted to a stout crossmember that was integral with the body.

The steering gear was simplified, and the steering box was now mounted behind the axle line, a change that significantly improved the car's passive safety by taking the forward end of the column well away from an accident, behind the axle line. Another bonus was the deletion of greasing points, the suspension being bushed with sealed-for-life units. The only greasing point to remain was on the propeller-shaft yoke.

At the rear there was still a live axle located by trailing arms, atop which were coil springs encircling the dampers. But there was a new system for providing extra axle location. Instead of the triangle of rods connecting the differential to the underside, there was now a robust T-piece to do the job. The crossbar of the T bolted between the chassis longitudinals ahead of the axle, and the stem ran rearwards to one side of the diff housing. This would prove a much better way of bracing the axle against tramp under hard acceleration. It also prevented rear-wheel steering, and was the reason for that quirky rear-end wiggle that Giulias flaunt when they're driven slowly over rough ground.

The wheels were 15in diameter, with shrouded drum brakes with three leading shoes, first used on the SS, rather than the paired shoes used on the

The twin-cam engine developed 92bhp in the Giulia TI using a single Solex carburettor. Its larger capacity of 1,570cc was achieved by boring and stroking, the latter necessitating a taller block. Despite the fact that the twin-cam was now eight years old, it remained a very sophisticated engine for the day with its all-alloy, wet-liner construction, twin cams, centrally-mounted plugs and sodium-filled exhaust valves. CAR MAGAZINE

mainstream Giuliettas. These were later replaced by a Dunlop disc brake system after Alfa had built about 22,000 Giulias. Another small but useful improvement was the relocation of the battery from the boot, where it often caused serious corrosion in the Giuliettas, to under the bonnet.

Inside, the car was noticeably less basic than the Giulietta saloon. The facia was decently padded, as was the rather baroque two-tone steering wheel, the passenger was provided with a huge 'panic handle' hung below the glovebox, and there was a reasonable stock of instruments that ran to a tachometer and an oil pressure gauge. The trim was of higher quality, too, but what really helped the cabin ambiance was the generous glazing and slender pillars which allowed a clear view out.

The switchgear was better organized, too. There was a group of white bakelite switches on the left and, more innovative still, stalks controlling the headlamps, including flashing, as well as the

indicators. Citroens were among the few cars of the time to use stalk controls. The thought behind this, the part-padded cabin and the repositioned steering box, were all evidence of Alfa's awareness of vehicle safety. But the Giulia's most significant safety feature was that its body was engineered with front and rear crush zones, the nose and tail deforming progressively in an accident in a bid to protect the passenger cell.

Crush zones weren't an Alfa invention – Mercedes was well advanced with this work – but cars engineered like this were depressingly rare in the early, pre-Ralph Nader Sixties. The Giulia itself wasn't going to stay rare for long, though. In its first year the 1600 Ti sold 13,873 examples, and 36,536 were built in 1963. The range soon expanded, the 92bhp 1600 Ti being joined by a Ti Super, which used the engine from the more highly tuned SS. This motor had a pair of twin-choke Webers strapped to its side, a higher compression ratio and revised cam profiles that pushed the

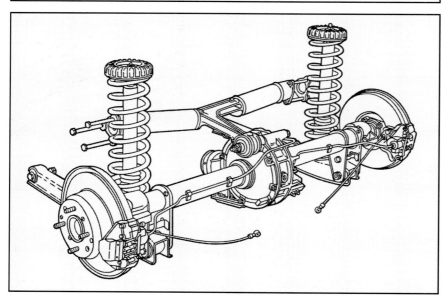

The Giulia's front suspension owed much to experience with the racing TZs. A coil-sprung double-wishbone arrangement, it was notable for the divided upper wishbone, allowing adjustment of the castor angle, and its freedom from greasing points. Though similar in principle to the Giulietta's set-up, it differed in having broader-based wishbones – which reduced camber change as the wheels rose and fell – the split upper wishbone mentioned and dampers mounted aft of the coil springs rather than within them. ALFA ROMEO ARCHIVES

The Giulia used a live rear axle, like the Giulietta, but it was located by a substantial T-piece, which better contained axle tramp, rather than an A-arm. Further location came from a pair of trailing arms, suspended by coil springs that encircled the dampers. Early Giulia saloons used drum brakes all round, discs coming after 22,000 cars had been built. ALFA ROMEO ARCHIVES

power output to 112bhp, generating a much juicier torque profile in the process. The Super was identifiable by the four-leaf clovers stuck to its front wings, which gave this rather unlikely looking saloon the air of a racer. The sportier character was rounded out with the transfer of the column shift to the floor, the junking of the front bench seat in favour of a pair of buckets, and a trio of round instrument dials in place of the mish-mash of strip speedo and small, circular tacho.

The dynamic mechanical qualities fuelled Alfa's urge to develop increasingly rapid versions of its

boxy saloon, which was clearly capable of harnessing plenty more than the 92bhp it came with in 1962. Road-testers of the day certainly thought the Giulia a well developed piece of kit on the open road. Here's Henry Manney III writing for *Road & Track* in June 1963: 'Avanti! Out into traffic and on to the Autostrada del Sole in the teeming rain, scarcely optimum conditions in which to take out an unfamiliar machine. Nevertheless, the good visibility of all four corners, excellent wiper spread, light steering and positive feeling of everything bred confidence, and even if the brakes snatched a bit, we soon treated wet as dry. This is an easier car to drive than the Giulietta, as well as many other cooking automobiles, and part of the credit must go to the strongly pulling and unfussed 1600 engine.' And: '. . . we bashed about the Futa Pass and found that the Giulia's combination of neutral attitude, improved lock, light steering without kickback, and reduced body roll really made enjoyable what could have been hard work.'

Needless to say, Manney found things he didn't like, not the least of which was bad propshaft rumble at certain engine speeds, but he reckoned the Giulia was 'a much better car than the Giulietta. Besides,' he added, 'it is nice having racing specifications in a family car.'

If the race car spec sounded good in a saloon, it was going to be even more tempting clothed in

Baroque steering wheel and a floor-mounted gearchange for this early Giulia TI. The instrumentation was all there, but rather messily laid out and styled, with a rectangular speedo and a circular rev-counter. CAR MAGAZINE

The rear end of the Giulia was not beautiful, but it held technical interest, the recessed panel of the Kamm tail reducing turbulence in the car's wake. The wrap-around screen helped reduce turbulence, too. The last of the series did without the broad channel in the bootlid. This is a Giulia 1300. ALFA ROMEO ARCHIVES

The dashboard of the 1965 Giulia Super was much tidier, featuring the large matched pair of speedo and tachometer typical of Alfa, together with wood veneer for the facia and a sports steering wheel. CAR MAGAZINE

Despite the unlikely looks, the Giulia saloon handled and rode well – many who drove both it and its sister Spider and GT models reckoned the saloon the best behaved of the trio. Given that all the chassis work was done on the saloon and that there was no fine tuning to take into account the shorter wheelbases and differing weights of the sportier models, perhaps this shouldn't be a surprise. CAR MAGAZINE

coupe and spider bodywork. And enthusiasts weren't going to have to wait too long for a sportier 105-series car to turn up. In the meantime, they had 92bhp 1600 versions of the original Giulietta Sprint and Spider to keep their Alfa desires alive, these models also gaining disc front brakes and a five-speed transmission to complement the more potent power plant.

They were renamed the Giulia Sprint and Spider, to mark the upgrade and allow Alfa to remain true to its policy of having among the most confusing model designations of any manufacturer in the world.

The finale for this Fifties sporting range was the arrival of a Veloce version of the Spider with a 112bhp engine, which produced a very brisk and entertaining car. But by now this was not enough – after all the Spider had been going for nearly 10 years, a long time for a fashion accessory to keep selling. Though Alfa built 7,107 1600-engined Sprints and 9,250 Spiders, the Veloce ragtop managed only another 1,091 sales. Something new was needed. And something new was coming.

CHAPTER 4

A Giulia for Romeos

The Giulia Sprint GT was designed in just two months by a 22-year-old who worked on it in the evenings during his national service. That man was Giorgetto Giugiaro, one of the most successful car designers of all time, whose record includes the De Tomaso Mangusta, the Alfasud, the Lotus Esprit, the VW Golf, the Fiat Panda and the Fiat Uno among the 80-plus cars he has created. The Giulia Sprint GT was one of his first designs, and it also happens to have been one of his most successful in the eyes of his critics, if not his own.

Giugiaro was instructed to shape the car by Nuccio Bertone, his employer at the time. Coachbuilders Bertone had produced the Sprint GT's predecessor, the Giulietta Sprint, not only designing the car for Alfa, but manufacturing it as well. It was the Giulietta that had taken Bertone into the big league, and it occupied an essential part of the coachbuilder's activity.

Since the Sprint had been such a success, it would have been surprising if Alfa Romeo hadn't once again enlisted Bertone's skills to produce a replacement. And it seemed obvious to Bertone himself that Giugiaro should produce some proposals for the new coupe. He might have been very young, but Giugiaro's was unquestionably an exceptional talent. He had worked in the Fiat design office and, having joined Bertone in 1959, had designed the Alfa 2000 Sprint (better known as the 2600) and the British Gordon-Keeble GT, which made its debut at the Geneva show in the spring of 1960.

Just after this, Giugiaro was drafted into national service, but Bertone pulled some strings to get him transferred to Bra, a tiny village about 50 kilometres from Turin, where the coachbuilders were based. Bertone rented his protege a room in a small hotel and provided him with a drawingboard and tools. From there two designs emerged which he worked up simultaneously on a pair of drawingboards – a one-off Ferrari 250 GT and the Giulia Sprint. He also had to knock up portraits of his officers during the day, the quid pro quo for staying in a hotel rather than the barracks.

Giugiaro worked on the project during March and April 1960 and, he explains, 'every Friday Nuccio Bertone came to see the car, because during the first three months of service it was not possible for new recruits to go home'. A scale model, also produced in the hotel room, came next, and Giugiaro remembers delivering it to Bertone in May 1960. He borrowed a rather battered Renault Dauphine from a fellow soldier and drove to Turin with the model on his lap. Despite this protection it was sufficiently damaged by the end of the journey that it took him quite a while to reassemble it. This was unquestionably the first Giulia Sprint restoration.

The effort was worth it, though, because Alfa's management liked Bertone's proposals so much that they decided to put the car into production, and with no alterations to the design, a rare thing in the car business, especially when the machine it was replacing had been so widely admired for its style.

On the other hand, the coachbuilders were not destined to manufacture Alfa's volume coupe this time. Success with the Giulietta Sprint and Alfa's growing popularity in general led to the decision to make the GT in-house. Not that this was an easy task for the company, which was finding

The pretty Giulia Sprint GT, like the Giulietta Sprint it replaced, was shaped by coachbuilders Bertone. It was longer and heavier, but had a shorter wheelbase than the old Sprint – curious, given the aim of providing more cabin room. Its 106bhp 1,570cc twin-cam engine gave it a stronger performance than all but the Veloce version of its predecessor. ALFA ROMEO ARCHIVES

The Sprint's rear was just as attractive as its front view, not least because of the unfussiness of the design. Its appeal lies in its basic shape, not in the decoration used to lift it, which was kept to a minimum. ALFA ROMEO ARCHIVES

itself increasingly squeezed in the Portello factory, where scope for expansion was limited because the surrounding area had been built up as Milan swelled. So the management elected to establish a new greenfield site at Arese, some way north of Milan, and the Sprint GT was to be the first car to emerge from that plant, though its mechanicals would still be supplied from Portello.

Though a very distinctive design, the Sprint bore quite a resemblance to the Gordon-Keeble and the Alfa 2600 Sprint, particularly in the roofline and the proportions of its bonnet and boot. Giugiaro was clearly developing a theme in

these three cars, one which he considers was most successfully resolved in the Giulia. But surprisingly, given the widespread admiration for the Sprint GT in the car design world, he doesn't think that highly of it now. 'It's a beautiful car for the period – not the best – but a good car. But it's not one of my favourite designs. I remember the mechanicals better than I do the car,' he grins, 'because I was driving Fiat 500s and 600s around at the time.'

One of the reasons for his indifferent feelings towards it now is to be found in the Giulia's nose. 'This was one of the first cars in which I tried to change a design habit,' he explains. 'It was the first attempt at the concept of inset headlamps, but this solution was not ideal.' Regulations forced separate indicators on Giugiaro, whose presence he did his best to disguise by building them into the leading edges of the front wings. But he clearly doesn't much like this set-up today, and reckons he didn't get the inset headlamp theme right until the VW Golf came along in 1974.

Despite Giugiaro's later lukewarm views towards the Sprint, it did a lot to establish him as a first-division designer, and it was to prove one of his most successful early designs in volume terms with almost 200,000 built by the time the car became obsolete in 1976. *Style Auto*, the Italian car design quarterly, certainly thought it a fine attempt.

Reviewing the Sprint GT in the winter 1964–65 issue shortly after the car made its debut at the Frankfurt show in late 1963, Yar Gregson wrote, in somewhat stilted English: 'The basic idea of the car still remains that which he (Bertone) had brought to realization in the Giulietta Sprint: to create a sporty, high-performance coupe which would nevertheless remain of universal use, as much at home on the autostrada as in city traffic or on mountain roads, and with enough comfort and room. This formula, particularly congenial to the frankly sporting character of the Alfa Romeo mechanicals and tested by racing success, has in the case of the Giulia GT reached a notable degree of balance: though not without faults, of which the most important is perhaps that it is not a real 4-seater, but it is one of the best examples of a fusion of contrasting requisites.'

Ironically, providing four seats was one of Alfa's major goals with this new project, yet the wheelbase was actually an inch shorter than the old Giulietta Sprint's, which can't have helped. Despite this, there was more room in the rear, but not space for the four adults Alfa initially claimed could comfortably be accommodated. About a year after the car came out, the company owned up, calling it a 2+2 instead.

Stylistically the GT scored highly, a fine achievement given that it was replacing one of the prettiest designs of the Fifties. Apart from its excellent proportions, the Sprint GT offered several novel design features which included recessed door handles, the inset headlamps already discussed, and the slender additional air intake created by the bonnet's raised leading edge.

But what gave the design real grace and

Giorgetto Giugiaro today. He designed the sprint while on national service, working from a hotel room. His proposals were so well-liked that they translated to production virtually unaltered. Giugiaro now heads ItalDesign, which he set up with engineer colleague Aldo Mantovani, with whom he designed the Alfasud. Giugiaro also facelifted the Giulietta Sprint and designed the Giulia Sprint's replacement, the Alfetta GT, as well as the Alfasud Sprint. ITALDESIGN

cohesion was the unbroken line that ran from nose to tail, neatly underlining the glasshouse on the way. Even today, there are few cars in which the wings, centre section and glass area are so tidily bound together. That brought the cohesion. The grace came from the subtle curve of that line as it dropped towards the Sprint's rump.

This approach meant that its wings completely blended into the body, rather than being the prominent objects that they had been in so many cars before. That may not sound remarkable today, when the same is true of virtually every modern car, but this was relatively fresh stuff in 1963. More unusual, even today, was the near-flat bonnet and the way the front wings sloped down to blend in with it. Being big and divorced from the front wings, the headlamps were distinctive, but the nose gained most of its character from the bold Alfa Romeo grille that encroached on the dihedral panel ahead of the bonnet.

The rear end was distinctive as well. Again, the

The Giulia Sprint's origins can be seen in the bigger 2600 Sprint, also designed by Bertone's Giorgetto Giugiaro, particularly in the roofline, the slender pillars and the glassiness of the cabin. ALFA ROMEO ARCHIVES

And in the Gordon-Keeble, also by Giugiaro, which shares much the same roof treatment and similar over-all proportioning. But the Giulia Sprint, the third version in the evolution of this shape, is the best resolved. RICHARD NEWTON

wings dipped down towards the boot which, like the bonnet, had its corners nearest the cabin lopped off, and the rear panel was recessed and contained a pair of large (for the day) lamp clusters.

There were simple bumpers that did without overriders, and no unnecessary trim to clutter up the flanks. What chrome there was traced the window outline. The only other decoration was a pair of badges on the lower part of the front wings – the Bertone badge, which was soon deleted to be replaced by a rectangle reading Disegno di Bertone, which stayed with the Giulia coupe to the end.

Inside, there was less evidence of flair. Giugiaro explains that it was a simple cabin, having been done at the very beginning of a period during which more attention to the interior would start to be paid. Nevertheless, the Giulia had a more ambitious and better stocked facia than the Giulietta Sprint, but it wasn't particularly radical. The driver viewed a quartet of Veglia instruments (and they were vague, too, the speedo being notorious for over-reading) through a black-rimmed steering wheel with three polished spokes.

The two larger dials, the rev-counter and speedometer, were flanked by a smaller pair of split gauges that registered oil pressure and fuel tank contents on the left and oil and water temperature on the right. There were warning lights for sidelights, dipped beam and main beam in the tachometer, and in the speedometer there was a blower warning light, a unique Alfa quirk. The ignition was on the left, and beneath this, under the facia, were a pair of tabs controlling the choke and hand throttle.

On the other side a trio of small paddle switches triggering panel lights, fan and the two-speed, clap-hands wipers snuggled beneath the far right gauge. This was in the original, left-hand-drive versions. Right-hand drive, which Alfa hadn't offered on the Giulietta Sprint, was an option this time, as it should have been if the firm was serious about exports to Britain and Australia.

Stalk controls from the Giulia saloon turned up again on the steering column, and the heater controls were shoved underneath the main dash panel, underlining the scant attention Italians tend to pay to these features. The passenger faced a modest lockable glovebox, there was a slot for a radio in the centre, and the whole ensemble was finished in a rather austere grey crackle paint.

Sill-to-sill carpeting, reclining bucket seats decently upholstered in leathercloth, fully trimmed doors and attractive aluminium kickplates lent the GT at least a hint of an upmarket air, but this was undermined by the bitty treatment of the heater controls and the lonely looking ashtray-cum-cigar lighter mounted just aft of the long gearlever.

But the cabin of a Giulia Sprint was a pleasant place to be, at least if you were up front, because there was plenty of room; the slim pillars heightened the airy feel and, if you were driving, you found most controls to be within easy reach.

What you were controlling was essentially a set of mechanicals hijacked intact from the Giulia 1600 Ti. The chief differences between the two were minor alterations to the twin-cam's tune and a cut-down propshaft, because the GT sat on a wheelbase of 93in, some 6in shorter than the saloon's. The point here, apart from making it stylistically easier to achieve a sporty look, was improving the car's agility. It also saved weight, the Sprint GT being some 110lb lighter than the saloon.

Like its brother, the GT sat on 15in perforated steel wheels and wore 155-section tyres, but this time there were disc brakes all round, the servo-assisted system having been developed for Alfa by Dunlop. The suspension was identical, however, consisting of the coil springs all round, double wishbones up front, trailing arms at the rear and that substantial T-piece to prevent sideways movement in the live rear axle. There was an anti-roll bar at the front, but none at the rear.

Though this suspension was similar in its fundamentals to the Giulietta's, it showed signs of

It takes a keen eye to differentiate the many versions of the Giulia Sprint, but earlier examples are identified by the air intake formed by the bonnet's leading edge – these cars are known as the step-front models. And this, a standard GT, is distinguished from the later Veloce model chiefly by its criss-cross grille. ALFA ROMEO ARCHIVES

Not as elegant as its exterior, the Sprint GT's interior was a strange mix, with rubber floor matting, a cheap-looking two-spoke steering wheel and a Fablon-covered dash, though early models had facias finished in grey crackle paint. However, there were some luxuries, including fully trimmed doors, plentiful instrumentation, a trip meter, the lockable glovebox and a hand throttle, seen with the choke knob below the ignition lock. ALFA ROMEO ARCHIVES

important lessons learned from the SZ racing programme – the front suspension, for example, was almost identical. There were advances on practical and safety fronts, too – greasing points had been reduced to three by using sealed ball-joints and, as on the Giulia saloon, redesigned and repositioned steering gear produced a very short column now that the steering box was behind the axle line, the result being limited rearwards column movement in accidents. When US safety regulations began appearing three years later, the Giulias needed little modification in this department to meet them, and again like the Giulia saloon, the Sprint was engineered with front and rear crush zones from the start.

The Sprint's engine was different from the units fitted to the two versions of the Giulia saloon that Alfa had launched so far, though it was of course a variation on the twin-cam four. Surprisingly, the GT did not get the most powerful version, the 112bhp unit fitted to the Sprint Speciale and the Ti Super saloon, but was equipped instead with a lower-compression (9:1 rather than 9.7:1) example. Twin downdraught carburettors were fitted and peak power, produced at 6,000rpm, was 106bhp, allowing a maximum speed of 112mph.

The transmission was five-speed, as for the saloon, but this time the change was floor-mounted from the start, the long gearlever being angled considerably for easy reach. The pedals

were floor-hinged in the case of clutch and accelerator (not uncommon in this era), though the throttle was pendant, its travel being limited by an adjustable circular steel stop screwed to the floor, a detail that lives on in modern Alfas. You could also control the idle speed with the hand throttle, a small metal tab under the dash, next to the similarly shaped choke with which it was easily confused.

Under the bonnet, the main visual change compared to the Giulia saloon was the twin carbs, rubber-mounted directly to the cylinder-head, and the air intake system, which called for a convoluted tube running across the engine bay to the air cleaner on the opposite side, an arrangement forced by the lower bonnet line. The jack was now banished to the boot, where the spare wheel was stored in a well under the floor next to the fuel tank, which was bolted into a sizeable aperture alongside.

The bootlid had no external catch, being released instead by a lockable lever mounted in the left-hand door jamb. Since Alfa never bothered to switch the location of this for right-hand-drive cars (except, strangely, for the CKD units built at Durban in South Africa), getting into the boot would always be a pain for British and Australian owners. The bonnet was also opened from the cabin by a lever on the far left of the facia, which again never switched position.

In spite of minor flaws like these, the Giulia

This profile view of the Sprint does much to show its beauty. Note the gentle curve of the line that runs from the front wing tops through the doors to the boot, and the recessed door handles, an advanced and rare feature for the day, although they were not easy to manipulate. Early cars had 15in wheels that suit less well than the 14in rims of later models. ALFA ROMEO ARCHIVES

Sprint GT was a very sophisticated car for the era. Coupes are common enough these days, for which we can thank Ford and its influential Capri, but in the early Sixties the choice of GT cars, in Europe at least, was depressingly limited. The best of them were immensely expensive, such as those coming from Ferrari, Aston Martin and Maserati, while the rest were either made up of machinery from small manufacturers like TVR, Elva, Reliant, or were obviously derived from

saloon car parentage, like the Lancia Flavia and the Peugeot 404 coupe. In 1964 the Alfa's main rivals in Britain were the Volvo 1800 S (1,778cc, 108bhp, 108mph), the Porsche 1600C (1,582cc, 75bhp, 105mph) and, unfortunately for the Italians, the startlingly cheap E-Type Jaguar (3,781cc, 265bhp, 111mph), which cost £1,913 as a coupe and actually undercut the £1,840 Sprint in soft-top form. For this reason the Sprints didn't exactly carpet Britain's roads – you'd have

This bonnet-less Sprint shows an engine little different from the Giulia saloon's other than in detail. Biggest difference is the twin carburettors and their intake plenum, which drew air from an air-cleaner on the other side of the engine. For the GT, the 1,570cc twin-cam engine produced 106bhp. In the far left of the engine bay can be seen the fuse box, which later was moved to within the cabin, where it was less susceptible to damage and damp. ALFA ROMEO ARCHIVES

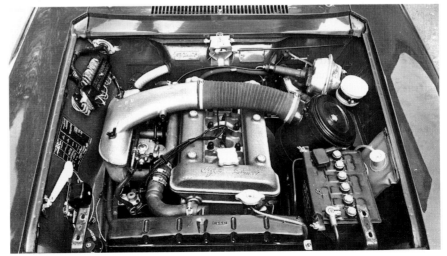

Apart from the raised leading edge of the bonnet, the Sprint's nose was unusual for its inset headlamps, a novelty that designer Giugaro felt didn't really work because the indicators and sidelights had to be incorporated outboard of them. The clap-hand wipers, on the other hand, were not so unusual in this era, though they're almost unseen today. ALFA ROMEO ARCHIVES

to want an Alfa pretty badly to pass over an E-Type – and that is presumably why the British motoring press never got around to road-testing the original version of the car.

The Americans got their Alfas at more reasonable prices, which doubtless encouraged *Road & Track* to get behind the wheel of a GT in late 1964. Their testers certainly enjoyed the car, enthusing over its five-speed gearbox, which they declared its piece de resistance, surpassing even the engine as a source of pleasure. Back then, of course, five-speeders were rarer than American cars that handled, which partly explains the praise. They also liked the cabin, 'correctly laid out for GT driving', the 'highly developed'

brakes, and the Sprint's 'ability to cover ground quickly without effort'.

Of the chassis they wrote, 'for those people who are convinced that independent rear suspension is essential for fast driving, the handling of the Alfa will come as a surprise, because the car is an excellent example of what can be done with a live axle if it is correctly located. Under certain conditions, there is a suspicion of the rear wheel steering one normally associates with swing-axle suspensions, but it never becomes exaggerated and is normally indiscernible. It is presumably caused by movement of the complete rear suspension in the big rubber bushes in which it is mounted.

'In a fast corner, the car is basically neutral although the application power in 3rd or 4th gears will cause it to understeer slightly. As one enters a turn at speed, there is a certain amount of roll oversteer initially, which seems to be accentuated by movement of the rear axle but, as soon as the car is positioned, this changes abruptly and the car becomes extremely stable.'

And of the engine: 'Second only to the transmission as a source of pleasure is the willingness of the engine. The tachometer goes to 8,000rpm with no red line and, due to the Webers, the manifolding and the exhaust system, there is little inclination for the engine to run out of breath. For maximum performance we shifted at 6,500rpm, but for normal fast touring 5,000rpm seems a good compromise.'

The article concluded with the old 'racing improves the breed' cliche (though it was probably less of one then), reckoning the Sprint GT to be conclusive proof of the truth of the saying.

It wasn't long before the Sprint began building on the reputation of the Giulietta, often being dubbed a baby Ferrari, which wasn't so far-fetched. It might only have been a four-cylinder 1600, but that all-alloy engine had twin cams, five main bearings, hemispherical combustion chambers, sodium-filled exhaust valves and duplex timing gear. Then there was the five-speed gearbox, the well-developed suspension, the servo-assisted disc brakes and the beautiful styling – all the stuff of race cars and Ferraris. It wasn't surprising that the GT began selling fast. And it was soon to be joined by a machine that would eventually become at least as desirable. But not at first.

CHAPTER 5

Car with no name

It may be hard to believe it today, but when it was launched in 1966 people reckoned the Alfa Spider was an ugly car. 'Cuttlefish' was one of the milder descriptions levelled at its shape, which, it seemed, was just too bold for people to get on with. They didn't like the scallops dug into its flanks, nor a nose and tail that had you wondering whether it was coming or going. More worrying still was that the public didn't like the new car as much as the machine it replaced. Customer resistance appeared to be Alfa's reward for having the courage to innovate.

Controversy like this often signposts avant garde design – really fresh shapes can take time to get used to, like Ford's Sierra and Citroen's DS – and the complaints were only fuelled by the fact that this new Spider replaced one that had been much admired for its style. That this latest version came from the same coachbuilders didn't do much to dispel the thought that this new Alfa might be a dud.

Comments culled from road tests of the time give you an idea. This was *Road & Track* in 1966: 'We found almost no disagreement among members of our staff about the appearance of the new model – no-one liked it as well as the Giulietta or the Giulia. One condemned it as a contrived design with meaningless styling gimmicks. Another said, "I think Pininfarina missed the ball this time".' Bill Boddy, in a *Motor Sport* road test of 1967, thought 'it could be called functional but its Pininfarina body is scarcely pretty'. With a reception like this, few would have bet that this car would be around 25 years later.

The Spider wasn't conceived as swiftly and decisively as the Sprint GT, evolving instead from a series of show cars, the earliest of which emerged 10 years before the finished machine arrived. Like its predecessor, the new Spider was to be the work of Pininfarina, just as Bertone got the job for the original Giulietta Sprint and its successor the Sprint GT. It would be the last car in which Battista Pininfarina, the coachbuilder's founder, had a direct hand. For that reason alone it is a landmark design. But no single name can be attributed with its shape, says Lorenzo Ramaciotti, Pininfarina's design chief today. Instead, he explains, the car grew from a series of show cars, and from the design culture that is Pininfarina.

First hints of what the new car would look like, though few can have known it at the time, were embodied in the Super Flow 1 show car of 1956 which, as the name suggests, was in part an aerodynamic study. Instantly identifiable as flamboyant Fifties design by its sizeable rear fins, the Super Flow had the Spider's side scallops, the Perspex-covered headlamps and a similar grille and air intake pattern. The slit-like air intakes that flanked the Alfa shield were highly adventurous for the day (just remember the grille size of the average saloon of the era) and were to turn up on the production machine. The Super Flow was an exceptionally glassy car, even having Perspex shrouds that covered the protruding headlights and the upper part of the front wings. Since the wings were cut away over the wheels, the shrouds would have been mud-spattered within yards. It was a flourish meant to be suggestive of an open-wheel design. Nevertheless, a vestige of the Perspex theme appeared on the Spider when it finally emerged with its

headlamps shrouded.

A second edition, unimaginatively labelled Super Flow 2, turned up later in the year. This version had lost the distinct nose and the silly front wings, but retained the channelled flanks and had a glass roof formed by curving the glass upper sections of the doors through 90 degrees to meet a narrow glass centre panel in the middle. It also had Perspex lamp covers.

Three years later came the Spider Super Sport, also known as the Tre S, in whose basic form you can see more of the production Spider. It, too, was based on a 6C 3500 chassis. This time the fins had gone, but the scallops stayed, and the car was a proper open-top. Like the Super Flow 2, it had a conventional nose that did without the Alfa shield. A year later a coupe version of this car was shown in Switzerland, though not at a motor show. In fact it was more than merely a hardtop version of the Tre S, featuring a less protuberant nose and less pronounced, asymmetrical scallops. The twin fairings aft of the seat backs had also been shorn off.

The final clue came at the Turin show in 1961 (still some five years away from production of the car) with the announcement of the Giulietta Spider Speciale Aerodinamica coupe which looked remarkably like the finished product. The major exterior differences were retractable headlamps,

front indicators let into the wings, less substantial bumpers and a rather more jutting centre grille. The prototype also had a glass rear window and a targa top. A year later, in 1962, there was a coupe version of this car which was basically the same except that it had a fuller rear screen, deeper side windows and a fixed roof, the whole of this unit raising a few inches at the front to allow easier access, a ludicrously impractical gimmick.

All six of these cars influenced the Spider to a greater or lesser extent, but the Spider Speciale was not to be Pininfarina's final word on the subject before the launch in 1966, the coachbuilders showing a 2600-based machine called the Cabriolet Speciale in October 1962 at Turin. A bigger, more angular car that nevertheless had considerable grace, it was shown to throw the opposition off the scent, and make the Spider's appearance four years later more of a surprise.

Why it took so long to appear in production is not completely clear, but the success of the car this prototype was built upon, the Giulietta Spider, is one reason, and the number of more important derivatives then under development is another. Whatever, it wasn't until the Geneva show in spring 1966 that the new Spider made its debut. It was not the best of them, either. Amazingly, Alfa hadn't given its new car a proper name, referring to it simply as the 1600 Spider, virtually the same

The first of the Pininfarina show cars from which the Spider was developed came in 1956. The Superflow Disco Volante was as remarkable for its fins as its glass canopy, but nothing was stranger than the Perspex shields that enclosed both the front wheels and the headlamps. But influences can be seen – the scallop along the sides, the rounded tail, the curved section of the flanks below the glass line and, though not evident in this shot, the integration of the shield grille. PININFARINA

Superflow 2 came later in the year, this time without the huge chunks of Perspex, though the material again shrouded the headlamps and was used to extend the fins vertically. The nose design drifted away from the production car and consisted of a simple, broad air intake. PININFARINA

Known as the Tre S, the Spider Super Sport was presented at the Geneva show in 1959. Its tail is very similar to the production car's, and the scallops are there, too, but the proportions are a little different. PININFARINA

A year later a hardtop version of the Tre S appeared, though there were detail differences, the fairing behind the seats having gone, the headlamps gaining shrouds and the scallops evolving. Like the Superflows, the Tre S coupe had a glass canopy that would have been thoroughly impractical, heating the cabin like a greenhouse even in mild sun. PININFARINA

label as used by its predecessor, the Giulia 1600 Spider. Not that the public was backward in coming forward with names of its own for the new machine, likening it to an octopus, a boat and a lentil seed, all thoughts inspired by its curious and, sadly, not much liked shape.

Critics thought it too contrived, both in form and detail, despite the fact that, viewed from above, the Spider possessed an immensely pleasing symmetry. But then, it is not every day that one sees cars from overhead. What was more likely to be noticed was the car's rather long overhangs, the corollary of the gently tapering nose and tail. Such a prickly reception must have come as quite a disappointment to Pininfarina after having invested a decade and six prototypes into this shape (plus the final Cabriolet Speciale as a smokescreen, to make seven), a ploy intended, among other things, to get the public used to a fresh form. But the Geneva show suggested that the public and the critics were going to need more time to learn how to love the Spider.

Yet there were subtleties in the design which the commentators seemed to pass by – the way in which the three-piece Alfa grille had been successfully incorporated into such a low nose, the way the rear lamps echoed the taper of the indent in the car's sides, the faired headlights and the tidiness of the hood, raised or lowered. More important, there were aerodynamic reasons for the fresh shape. It was one of the first production cars to flaunt such extreme curvature beneath the

window line though it was the Jaguar E-Type that won that race.

It wasn't the curvature that aided the car's passage through the air so much as the scallops cut in its flanks, which enhanced directional stability in side winds by drawing air over the car more effectively, a fact discovered after many hours of work in the wind-tunnel with the earlier prototypes.

Reasons for the emphasis on aerodynamic performance stemmed from Alfa's interest in this field during the Fifties. The company was one of the first manufacturers to understand the

importance of air penetration (along with Citroen and Panhard), a preoccupation that spawned the BAT cars, a series of streamlined experimental cars initiated by chief engineer Satta, who had a degree in aeronautical engineering. The BAT cars never made series production – they weren't meant to – but Satta ensured that what the company learned was actually incorporated into products the public could buy. The Spider was just one of them.

Controversy invaded the new roadster's cabin, too. The painted dash looked cheap, despite the padded mouldings at top and bottom, and the rubber mats were also a bit utility, even if they were sensible. But the Spider was not under-equipped. It had a pair of carefully shaped reclining seats that provided better than average comfort, and a particularly fine set of instruments dominated the cabin architecture.

The driver faced a giant-sized speedometer and rev-counter, their needles and markings arranged so that the critical ranges were closest to the sight line. Between this pair were warning lights for sidelights, main beam and indicators, and a

warning for the alternator and a heater fan indicator were sunk in the dials themselves. In the centre of the dash were three smaller instruments for fuel tank contents, oil pressure and water temperature, each mounted on a chrome bezel angling them towards the driver. Beneath these was a Pininfarina-badged blanking plate for the radio, and either side of that were toggle switches for the single-speed, clap-hands wipers and the blower.

A third toggle outboard of the main instrument binnacle lit the panel lights. Washers were triggered by a foot-operated button to one side of the floor-hinged pedals (the wipers swept simultaneously) and, as on the GT coupe, a pair of tab levers under the facia controlled the choke and hand throttle. Behind the three-spoke alloy and plastic wheel hid the same stalks fitted to the Giulia saloon and GT, operating indicators, sidelights and headlamps.

At the extremities of the dash were a pair of air vents, a surprise given that the coupe, which arguably needed them more, had to do without this luxury. Face-level ventilation was a rarity even in the mid-Sixties, and the Spider's

Shortly after the open car, Pininfarina wheeled out a hardtop version, the roof of which could be raised a few inches at the forward edge to create more headroom on entry. An expensive solution that did little to solve a minor problem. PININFARINA

designers might well have been influenced by the Triumph TR4, which was the first production car to offer this feature. Heater controls were hung under the dash, the two sliding levers controlling air volume and temperature. Air direction was controlled by a flap over the transmission tunnel.

Aft of the black-knobbed gearlever, identical to the GT's, was the same combination ashtray and cigar lighter, one of the items that marked the car as rather more upmarket than some of its stripped-out (and mostly British) competition. It is hard to think of a cigar lighter as a luxury in an era when electric windows and central locking are fairly mundane, but the age when the Japanese forced the level of standard equipment ever higher had yet to be reached. So the fact that the Spider came with twin sun visors, a dipping mirror, a door-operated courtesy light (neatly installed in the rear-view mirror moulding), fully trimmed doors, quarter-lights and reclining seats marked it out as a comprehensively kitted car, and never mind those rubber mats.

It was also available from the start with an optional Pininfarina-designed hardtop, a hefty glassfibre lid which, despite its straight-line styling, looked a lot better than winter roofs of rival sports cars. Not many were sold, though, because it added another 4% to the price of a car that wasn't cheap in the first place. This is why hardtops are difficult to come by today.

Another reason was that the standard hood was so good in the first place. Taut, tidy and waterproof, more than a quarter of a century later it remains an object lesson in how these things should be done. That's because it was so simple to manipulate. There were no studs to undo, no zips to pull or hidden clips to release – just operate a couple of catches behind the sun visors and the hood, permanently attached to its frame irons, folded back behind you. A couple of leather straps tied the catches down to stop the rattling, and if you could be bothered to attach it, there was a

tonneau to cover the folded canvas and tidy the looks. But that wasn't really needed because the hood dropped virtually below waistline anyway.

This robbed space from behind the seats, but only sadists would suggest that anyone could actually ride in the well aft of the front buckets – it might have offered more room than some other sportscars, but not enough for human habitation. You could fit luggage in, though, even when the hood was furled. Not that the boot was meanly dimensioned. Long, wide, but rather shallow, it nevertheless offered a big enough dumping ground for a fortnight's touring holiday to be a serious proposition. As on the GT, the bootlid was released by a lockable lever in the left-hand door jamb. Luggage shared the boot with the spare wheel, mounted in a well beneath a rubber mat, with the fuel tank to one side of it, and the jack, which was clamped to the forward bulkhead.

The spacious boot was the result of the Spider's substantial rear overhang, a feature of its architecture at the front end, too. Despite having a wheelbase nearly 5in shorter than the Giulia GT's, its overall length was 167.3in, over 6in more. That promised slightly more agile handling than the coupe could offer (a shorter wheelbase tends to make directional changes easier), though mechanically the two were very similar.

This meant it had double wishbones, coil springs and an anti-roll bar at the front, and trailing arms, coils and the hefty T-shaped locating arm at the rear. There was a five-speed gearbox as standard – unknown on similarly priced sportsters, which at best would offer an optional, and probably unreliable, overdrive – recirculating-ball steering and disc brakes all round, though this time there was no servo. This was curious, because the 2,181lb Spider actually weighed 91lb more than its sister GT, and would theoretically have demanded more effort to stop – the difference probably came about because the GT was homologated as a four-seater.

The Spider's main mechanical alteration from the Giulia GT lay with its engine, however. It was substantially the same – a four-cylinder 1,570cc engine with five main bearings, twin cams and of all-alloy construction – but this time there was more power than the 106bhp offered in the GT, though the increase was not great, output being lifted to 109bhp. Oddly enough this meant that it was fractionally less powerful than the ultimate version of its predecessor, the 1600 Spider Veloce, which mustered 112bhp thanks to a higher compression ratio.

However, that didn't stop the new car from being quicker, with a 115mph top speed, and more flexible, too, because it delivered a fatter torque curve. The underbonnet layout was much the same as the GT's, this particular application of the twin-cam being identifiable by the twin carburettors' massive alloy plenum chamber and the convoluted fabric tube that directed air to them from a cylindrical air filter.

This, then, was a sophisticated confection of

It might look great today, but when it first appeared the public cared little for the new Spider, likening it to various forms of inelegant sea-life and crops. Few bought one, despite Pininfarina's efforts to curry favour with all those prototypes. ALFA ROMEO OWNERS CLUB

Simple but well-equipped, the Spider's dash presented the important information – speed and revs – boldly, while the minor gauges, angled towards the driver, were almost as clear. Note that the rev-counter's red paint is positioned where it is most easily seen. The dash looked cheap with its metal finish, though, and the heater controls were rather untidily located.

mechanicals that would have pleased any enthusiast to own, even if it was enveloped in controversial bodywork. All the Spider lacked was a name. Bereft of ideas of its own, Alfa announced a competition to find one on the day it announced the car, the winner collecting a Spider as a prize.

These tactics attracted a barrage of suggestions (over 140,000 in 10 months) and, needless to say, a sizeable collection of the strange and stupid. Best of these were Hitler, Shakespeare, Stalin and Sputnik, as well as Edelweiss, Pizza, Al Capone and Zeus. Slightly more sensible were Piranha, Panther, Leopard and Wolf, but the winning entry came from one Guidobaldi Trionfi from Brescia, whose suggestion of Duetto was pleasingly euphonious and emphasized the Spider's two seats and twin cams. In English, at

least, this seems a fine name, but to Italians it apparently sounds slightly crass, which could be why Alfa never bothered tooling up a Duetto badge for the car.

Whatever people's thoughts on the Spider's name and appearance, there was no doubt that enthusiasts liked driving the thing. Praise in the press was near-universal. Here's *Road & Track* again, from the same test that criticized the car's shape: 'If no-one of the staff was wild about the Duetto's appearance, exactly the opposite was true about driving the car. Everybody loved it. The overall impression is one of great responsiveness, and the feeling that the car is an extension of the driver at the controls is unmistakably clear. The steering is excellent – light, accurate and among the best we've ever encountered in any car. We've already led three

Shiny vinyl seats, and they don't look very supportive, either, though they were better than many of the day – they also reclined. The tunnel was carpeted, yet the footwells were covered with rubber mats. The doors were fully trimmed, but were without armrests. The cabin was roomy for two, not too draughty, and provided some stowage behind the seats.

In 1966, the year of its launch, a trio of Spiders was displayed aboard the Raffaello during a crossing to the US designed to promote the products of Finmeccanica, of which Alfa Romeo was a part. Two passengers ordered a pair of Spiders, and those who drove the cars on deck were given certificates to say they had driven a car on the high seas. Heady stuff. ALFA ROMEO ARCHIVES

cheers for the gearbox, and except to add that 5th is actually overdrive and gives the car a long-legged, easy-running cruising speed, there's little that we can add.

'It might be superfluous to add that the Duetto seems to be at its very best on winding roads. All Alfas are. The Duetto sits much flatter in the turns than did the Giulietta or Giulia and there is a noticeable lessening of body lean.' Winding up, the magazine suggested that 'all politicians be required to drive one a thousand miles or so before considering themselves qualified for making speeches about what an automobile ought to be'.

British magazines had to wait longer to get right-hand-drive Spiders to try, getting their first taste of the car at an international launch on Lake Garda. *CAR Magazine*'s George Bishop was one of the samplers. 'About 20 examples in red, white, blue and British Racing Green (vive le common market) were lined up on the private quay of the Hotel Astoria under black plastic sheets the night before the race . . . sorry, test day. Alfa may not make all that many cars –

around 70,000 a year – but by Allah they make them well and know how to present them to the press. On the morning of the assay each car was started by a blue-overalled mechanic and brought to the start-line warmed up and ready to go. Drivers were matched in pairs and, after signing a blood-chit, assigned to a numbered car, which avoided all this "After You Claude and I'm Not Riding With 'Im" lark.'

The group was also shown the new Giulia Sprint GT Veloce (more about that later) which brought on some interesting comparisons. 'Appearancewise we think the Spider (by Pininfarina) is uglier than the GT (by Bertone), spoilt by a groove along the side. This poses a problem for the window-shopper, since the Spider handles better and feels tauter and more of a piece. So do you marry the ugly sister with the money, or settle for honeysuckle with the pretty poor one? We said earlier, take Spider-con-hardtop, which gives a dry head.'

Bishop added: 'You have to push damned hard to break either end away (we were on Xs) and all

The winner of Alfa Romeo's competition to give the Spider a name, Guidobaldo Trionfi, gets his prize of a car from Giuseppe Luraghi, president of Alfa. There were 140,501 entries, Baldi's being Duetto. ALFA ROMEO ARCHIVES

Pininfarina's optional hardtop made the Spider more of a winter proposition, though it did little to enhance the car's elegance. It was an expensive extra, and so a rare find today. ALFA ROMEO ARCHIVES

in all it struck us – both types that is – as a nice car(s). In England they cost nearly twice the Italian price . . . but our domestic makers don't offer a comparable machine which is small, looks nice and performs well. An Elan is the nearest thing but doesn't have the luxury-type comfort

and solidity – the they-don't-build-them-like-that-any-more feel.' By which you can gather that Bishop rather enjoyed his early forays in these Italian semi-exotics.

But it would be almost a year before a British magazine – *Motor* – got a right-hand-drive Spider

Like its Sprint GT brother, the Spider did not need to rely on decoration to lift it. The smooth ovoid was broken only by the scallops along its sides, while virtually every accessory was shaped to fit the body's form – the headlamps faired in to allow the front wings to finish less abruptly, the rear lamps continued the shape of the fenders, and the bumpers recessed to the point where they provided little protection against damage. ALFA ROMEO ARCHIVES

to put through a full work-out at the MIRA test track. They got 111.1mph from the car, and a 0–60mph time of 11.2sec. With figures like these the Alfa didn't fare too well against the cars in the magazine's comparison boxes (a Healey 3000, Reliant Scimitar, Lotus Elan, Marcos 1800 and an E-Type Jaguar), all of which were faster and, bar the Jag, cheaper.

But that didn't stop the testers liking the car. This is what they had to say about the Duetto's handling: 'Despite fairly low gearing (for a sports car) the steering provides a superb feel of the road with occasional kickback on bumpy surfaces as the only penalty. It is probably because of this feel that the characteristics of the car are a good example of the distinction between handling and roadholding: its roadholding is certainly good by sports car standards, but its handling is really outstanding – the Duetto is a supremely chuckable car. On dry surfaces it goes round corners in a consistent stable understeer under power and there is little attitude change if circumstances force you to lift off. When trying really hard there is moderate roll and some tyre squeal and the car eventually reaches a curious (and typically Alfa) rocking motion but without in any way feeling unsafe or attempting to break away rapidly at either end. Bumpy surfaces do not deflect the Duetto very much during hard cornering, and unlike quite a few modern sports

cars, it runs arrow straight at high speeds', added the testers.

Motor also liked the transmission, explaining that though 'five-speed gearboxes are becoming increasingly common, as yet no more than a handful of the world's most expensive cars use one besides the volume-produced Porsche and Alfa. It is not merely in having a five-speed gearbox that the Duetto is head and shoulders above most other sports cars, but in having a five-speed gearbox that is so superbly pleasant to use. With unbeatable synchromesh the changes are light, precise and of the hot-knife-through-butter type.'

The relative novelty of the five-speeder must have been the reason it earned more type than the engine in *Motor*'s test, though they enjoyed the twin-cam, too, commenting that once a disturbing rattliness during warm-up had passed, 'the engine is reasonably quiet up to about 3,000rpm, above which it develops a hard, purposeful note. It pulls well from surprisingly low speeds in the very high top gear and has commendable smoothness right up to the tachometer limit of 6,200rpm – and after a brief acquaintance with the car it seems natural to use all these revs whenever the opportunity arises.'

The Spider also picked up points 'over most other genuine sports cars in having a softer and more comfortable ride' and for having 'excellent seats with reclining backs which provide good lateral and lumbar support', but lost some for a driving position favouring people of the long-arm, short-leg variety and for not having enough rearward seat travel. *Motor* also carped about mediocre visibility, the extremities of the body being hard to see and the wiper sweep inadequate. Curiously they didn't criticize the hood in this respect, whereas other magazines reckoned its lack of rear side windows a serious flaw.

But it was obvious that whatever their views about its style, no-one failed to enjoy the way the Spider went. It might not have started life with an identity, but this new Alfa wasn't short of character.

Just the kind of environment that cuts short a Spider's life; the under-protected bodywork was very vulnerable to salt and damp, elements the British climate so readily provides. This picture reveals another perpetual Spider problem, though more minor – where to put the front number-plate, which has never had a proper home. ALFA ROMEO ARCHIVES

CHAPTER 6

More models, more speed

It didn't take Alfa long to start the further development of the new Giulias, and the saloon proliferated particularly swiftly. The company was beginning to learn about marketing, and in particular about making the best use of its own talents. Chief among these was making sporty cars sportier, and going racing. By now Alfa's competition efforts had switched from Formula One to saloon car racing, where it had piled up dozens of victories, first with the petite and pretty SZ, which was based on the Giulietta Sprint, and then with the highly specialized TZs, cars built up around an alloy birdcage frame. They are among the most desirable and exotic of the postwar Alfas, yet they share much in common with the road cars. You can read more about the exotic make-up of these machines in Chapter 10.

Closer still to showroom machines were the GTAs. They were born of Alfa's decision to go after silverware in the Group 2 Touring class, when the rules became flexible enough to allow a production car to form the basis of a racer rather than demanding a special like the TZ. Not that the GTAs were ordinary cars. They might have looked much the same as the Sprint GT, but they had a pretty ambitious mechanical specification which included alloy body panels, modified suspension and a twin-plug head for the twin-cam engine, boosting the 1600's power to 115bhp at 6,000rpm in road-going form. For the track, this fiery powerplant could deliver 170bhp at 7,500rpm.

Grunt like this, coupled to a body from which 449lb had been pared, meant electric performance and, very soon, cupboard-loads of trophies for the Carlo Chiti-run Autodelta outfit that controlled Alfa's competition exploits. The GTAs would win for Alfa Romeo the European Touring Car Championship in 1966, '67 and '68, besides countless other prizes. Chapter 11, which deals with Alfa's racing adventures, covers this in more detail.

If the GTA was an unusual development of the Sprint, which at this time was still only available in one guise, what came next was rather strange, and it was rapidly followed by a machine that was downright bizarre. Apart from their mechanicals, just about all they had in common was a soft-top because one was a four-seater open tourer and the other a retro car whose Thirties style was built on the Giulia's modern mechanicals.

The conversion of the Sprint GT into a GTC (the C was for cabriolet) was carried out by Touring, the long-established coachbuilders who had created numerous beautiful bodies for Alfa in the past. Since it was never designed as a convertible, considerable strengthening of the lower half of the coupe had to be effected in order to compensate for the absence of a roof and rear pillars. Most of this buttressing was hidden, but the footwells were visibly constricted by the extra sheet metal added at the sides, and the backrest of the rear seat was narrower to create space for storage of the hood mechanism. Since the hood folded virtually flush with the GT's rear end, a compartment into which it could be folded was created aft of the rear seat, which reduced the size of the boot. The bootlid, however, became larger. The rear side windows were altered, too, winding out of sight like the door glasses (also unique to the GTC) to provide completely open motoring.

Despite the large amount of fabric involved, the GTC's hood, which was tied to the front cantrail

It looked much the same as a standard Giulia Sprint, but the GTA (A for allegerita, meaning lightened) was much altered, the exterior body panels being made from aluminium and riveted to the steel under-structure to save weight. The engine, a twin-plug version of the 1600 twin-cam, produced 115bhp in untuned guise and race prepared it could turn out 170bhp. ALFA ROMEO ARCHIVES

by a pair of clamps, was easy to fold away, and it came with a tonneau cover to tidy it once stowed. There was also an optional hardtop, a colossal chunk of steel that was usually painted in a contrasting colour. Wind down the side windows and there was a pillarless coupe for the cooler seasons. However, very few of these can have been manufactured, not least because so few GTCs were built. One reason was Touring's limited capacity and another was the car's high price, but what must have effectively finished it off was the arrival of the Spider convertible. The market for four-seater ragtops had not developed to the pitch it has today, and in any case room at the rear was really tight unless those up front were prepared to slide their seats well forward.

The GTC was liked well enough by the press, though, who tried it just before its debut at the 1965 Geneva show. *Autocar* reported: 'Travelling in the back with the hood down and neatly hidden under a tonneau cover, we found the car surprisingly quiet but rather draughty round the back of the neck.' They reckoned 'it handled impeccably with all the precision and predictable behaviour that have kept Alfa models so well established in sports car markets throughout the world', and found that 'with the hood up.....there

is hardly any loss of headroom compared with the closed coupe and vision is not impaired'.

The magazine's biggest reservation was that 'the car we drove did not feel entirely rigid, and there was some scuttle shake while travelling over rough parts'. Other journalists found the same problem. Given the area that Touring's tinsnips had opened up, it was no surprise that the body engineers were unable to prevent the shell shivering over bumpy terrain; to do so would have added too much weight and complexity.

If the GTC was rare (it certainly would be in Britain because only 99 were made with right-hand drive) the Zagato 4R, which appeared a month later in April 1965, would be rarer still, garnering the distinction of being the least common Giulia derivative of all. Just 92 cars were built between 1966 and 1968.

The idea behind this strange machine came from the Italian magazine *Quattroruote* (hence the 4R of its name), which reckoned that the running gear of a Giulia 1600 Ti might make the basis of a modern replica of the 1750 Gran Sport of the 1930s. Alfa was persuaded to take up the idea, and modified the proportions by lengthening the wheelbase and narrowing the track to recreate more closely the dimensions of the original.

The GTA was identifiable by its close mesh grille, the lack of any grille at all between headlamps and indicators, the green cloverleaf triangle on the front wings, delicate little door handles, the absence of hubcaps, and another cloverleaf on the rear panel. Competition versions, prepared by Alfa's racing arm Autodelta, featured additional air intakes behind the front bumper. TIM WREN

Meanwhile, Zagato was enlisted to build the body, an appropriate choice since the Milanese coachbuilder had fabricated the bodywork of the original 1750s. The 4R was built up on a tubular frame and clothed in hand-beaten panels that resembled the 1750's quite closely. Stylistically, the most unsatisfactory elements were the wheels, which were of insufficient diameter, but in other respects the 4R was not too far off.

It should have been a brilliant success, and today, perhaps, it might have been, but back in the 1960s it was seen as a cheapskate counterfeit, despite the huge amount of work that went into each one. The car drove well, too. Here is *Autocar* again: 'You sit there like God in his Heaven, with a superb view of everything around you; there are no screen pillars to obscure your view, and the wind whistles past your ears, making certain that in no circumstances whatever do you feel drowsy. The steering, though moderately low-geared with 3.5 turns from lock to lock, is splendidly quick and precise, the car answering almost to tightenings or slackenings of one's grip, like a racing car. One has, therefore, almost to lean it through fast bends. It shows no trace of roll on corners, nor does it seem to over- or understeer, being as well balanced as any car which I have driven.'

Few companies other than Morgan could have produced a replica like this, and the Malvern company certainly would not have been able to endow their beast with manners that were so appealingly ancient and modern. That Alfa could capture some of a Thirties flavour in the way the 4R drove was partly down to the fact that the

The rare GTC (C for cabriolet), a Sprint GT converted by coachbuilders Touring. Much strengthening of the floor and sill areas was needed to compensate for the rigidity lost through the removal of the roof, despite which the car still suffered serious scuttle shake. Though this shot appears to reveal room for four, space in the back was cramped. ALFA ROMEO ARCHIVES

Despite the fact that it was never intended as a convertible, the GTC made an elegant machine, helped by the fact that its hood folded very compactly, in contrast to those of many modern cabriolets, and that its side windows wound right out of sight. It was available optionally with a hardtop. ALFA ROMEO ARCHIVES

Giulia's mechanicals had directly evolved from the 1750's running gear, and having Zagato build the body in the same way as it had manufactured the original's ought to have lent the 4R the authenticity it needed to succeed. However, after such a disappointment, it is hard to imagine Alfa ever embarking on such an adventure again, even if the Japanese (or at least Nissan) have followed a similar route, seemingly successfully, with their S-Cargo, Pao and Figaro retro cars.

Approximately a year after the 4R, the GTC and the GTA were unveiled, Alfa at last introduced a quicker version of the Sprint GT. The GT Veloce made its debut at the 1966 Geneva show along with the new Spider, whose 109bhp engine it shared. An extra 3bhp may not sound much, but the Veloce motor gained much more in maximum torque, and in the shape of its torque curve, over the GT's 106bhp unit. Peak torque was now 115lb/ft compared with 103lb/ft, and it arrived earlier, at 2,800rpm instead of 3,000rpm.

These changes had been achieved with minimal alteration to the 1,570cc engine. There were porting changes and the inlet valves had grown from 35mm to 37mm in diameter, but the exhaust valves were unchanged at 31mm. The cams had different profiles to increase valve lift, but the compression ratio remained at 9:1 and the carburettors were usually Weber 40 DCOEs, as for the GT, though with slightly altered jetting. None of these changes was visible under the bonnet, the engine bay looking to be identical to

The GTC's side glass was unique to the model, as was its bigger bootlid. The hood was easy to fold away in spite of its size. ALFA ROMEO ARCHIVES

the GT's when the lid was raised.

Exterior changes were also minimal. The chief identifying feature was the grille, which was now composed of three horizontal chrome slats over fine black mesh to flank the famous shield instead of the chrome grid effect of the plain GT. At the back end there was a chrome Veloce script to the right of the number-plate plinth on the rear panel, and

The facia of the GTC was identical to the Sprint GT's, being finished in crackle grey paint. Just visible, to the sides of the footwells, is evidence of the considerable extra buttressing the body needed to make up some of the strength lost by slicing off the roof. ALFA ROMEO ARCHIVES

at the base of the rear pillars were a pair of quadrifoglio badges providing subtle identification from the side. Wheels, hubcaps and tyres (155-15s) remained the same, as did all the sheet metal.

Inside, alterations were similarly limited. The most important change was a real improvement, for enthusiasts at least, because the rather flat front seats of the GT were replaced by a pair of bucket seats whose backrests wrapped round the torso pretty convincingly. The facia was also altered, if not necessarily improved, by being covered in wood-effect Fablon, but there were no extra gauges or controls.

Curiously, these alterations appeared to have added 154lb to the car, which was much more than might have been expected, but the weight increase probably had as much to do with production modifications to the Sprint since its launch as to its blossoming into a Veloce. According to most vehicle engineers a car invariably gains weight through its life as processes and components are subtly changed.

This might well explain the rather limited on-paper improvement to the Sprint's performance. Few magazines managed to test both the GT and the GT Veloce, but *Road & Track* managed to do so. Its testers certainly improved on the 0–50mph time, which fell by a second to 7.2sec, but the 10.5sec time for 0–60mph was only a tenth better. The standing quarter-mile improved from 18.5sec to 17.6sec, but all the acceleration times after

60mph were swifter in the original GT, which posted a 0–100mph time of 31.8sec compared with the Veloce's 35.5sec.

Road & Track complained of clutch slip in the test Veloce, however, and perhaps they tested it on a more windy day, which would explain the longer high-speed times. Minor disappointments like this, though, did little to dampen their enthusiasm for the little coupe, their report revealing that 'most staff members managed to find impeccable reasons either to renew their acquaintance or to see what they had missed three years ago. As testing proceeded, nearly every driver had praise for the car; a rather startling unanimity of opinion'.

The test report explained that 'the reasons for this broad spectrum of appeal are both simple and complex. They boil down to a machine carefully designed to become an extension of the human body, satisfying its wishes and amplifying its physical actions with a minimum of mechanical interference. This is no uncommon goal for automobile designers, of course, but the scarcity of such vehicles indicates the extreme difficulty of execution'.

Road & Track had discovered the essence of a good Alfa here, the things Satta talked about in that quote at the beginning of this book. That is part of what makes Alfas so special. The parts that made this Sprint GT Veloce special were many, and included its engine, its gearbox, its handling,

The Zagato 4R was inspired by the Italian magazine *Quattroruote*, the idea being to create a modern replica of the 1750 of the Thirties. It produced a terrific toy, but one that was misunderstood as a cheap counterfeit. Only 92 were built, but it is easy to imagine it being a success today. ZAGATO

steering and brakes and its seats. Here are a few more quotes to demonstrate the breadth of the car's appeal: 'The engine starts quickly, idles quietly and outside of a tendency to foul plugs in easy running it is remarkably vice-free for a unit with a power output of over 1.2bhp/cu in.

'Our great enjoyment of the transmission has brought forth emconiums in the past and undoubtedly will again. This all-but-faultless unit gives the driver a control of gear ratios very nearly as flexible, swift and effortless as the thought of shifting itself.'

As ever with an Italian car, the driving position didn't score with everyone, though: 'Most drivers, ranging through both extremes of the height scale, could find excellent accommodation for operating the car easily and with long-haul comfort. Others decided that their arm and leg length were outside the Italian norm, requiring some to adopt an indecorous knee-spraddle around the steering wheel and a few to resort to an unstylish elbow-cock.'

The seats did better: 'The new Alfa swept-around bucket seat, however, earned complete – or nearly complete – approval . . . . The configuration of the front seats is very good, giving complete lateral support during brisk driving, yet freedom for necessary body action. Seat travel is long and seat-back rake is variable through a considerable arc by use of a large, positive-acting knob at the side.'

And so did the brakes: 'A series of hard stops from 60mph showed exactly the result we expected from a well-designed disc system: sustained braking power with very little increase in pedal effort, and no loss of control.'

The test concluded: 'As one of the last sporting redoubts of the live rear axle, Alfa maintains its position with powerful ammunition indeed. The combination of light, precise steering and controllable understeer through almost any road condition makes it an easy, safe and enjoyable car for the novice, as well as a source of continuing exhilaration to the skilled driver.'

There was no less enthusiasm on the European side of the Atlantic to judge by *Autosport*'s impressions of the Veloce in February 1967. Tester Patrick McNally found that 'surprisingly there is simply no comparison between the GT and the GTV, for the very minor alterations make the Veloce a much better car'. He certainly enjoyed the engine, which 'revs happily to well over 7,000rpm, sounding really strong at the top end, like all the best Italian machinery.

'One of the most outstanding features of the Veloce is that the increase in horsepower has been obtained without a detrimental effect on flexibility. The new valve timing makes the most of the refined twin-Weber carburation induction system and, if anything, the engine is just as flexible as that of the ordinary Giulia.'

McNally had much to say about the Veloce's manners: 'Without doubt the best feature of the car is the rapport which exists between car and driver. This feeling of being part of the car enables the driver to throw the car about with much abandon, especially with the right-hand-drive model, where the gearbox tunnel provides a great deal of support for the left leg. When driving fast it is very necessary to have the maximum body support so that the hands can be used not to brace oneself but to twiddle the wheel

The Sprint GT Veloce gained 3bhp over the standard GT and noticeably improved driveability, besides a package of subtle changes. ALFA ROMEO ARCHIVES

Most obvious here is the new three-slat chrome grille with its mesh backing, the main alteration at the front. ALFA ROMEO OWNERS CLUB

– which is the idea anyway.

'The suspension, considering it the combination of live rear axle and fully independent front suspension, is exceptionally good and the Veloce goes through corners sitting down well on the road with the minimum of the characteristic Alfa body roll. The roadholding in the dry is excellent and for a production car the understeer is minimal. Although the GTV could never be described as an oversteerer, the lock over direction has been reduced considerably. Most cars which have near-neutral handling tend to be very twitchy and lack straight-line stability, but this is not the case with the Veloce.'

McNally unearthed what would become a familiar GTV failing, though, when he explained: 'When cornering really hard the inside rear wheel can be made to leave the ground, and in the absence of a power-lock diff this can have interesting effects.' He did better with his test car than *Road & Track* when it came to performance figures, the Veloce turning in a 0–60mph time of 10.3sec and a top speed of 116.3mph.

CAR Magazine also enjoyed a session with the

GTV in late 1967, by which time the model was 18 months old. '. . . the GTV feels absolutely right from the moment you take the wheel. It is a moderately sporting version of the basic Bertone Sprint coupe with its 1,600cc engine tickled to produce more revs and four more bhp than the Giulia Super saloon, placing it in output roughly between a Lotus Elan and an Elan S/E. But it remains a civilized machine, quiet and smooth at touring speeds and with enough room in the shapely body to accommodate three adults or a family with two children of almost any age. The seats wrap round more than in any other Alfa except the racing GTA, the controls are as always so perfectly placed that you can hardly understand what the expression means until you have tried them, there is still too little legroom, and the dashboard has a mock-wood finish that will endear it to very few even though the instruments are housed in lovely big round dials. On the road, there is an immediate impression not so much of the urge as of smooth, sustained, politely controlled power that acts in concert with five perfectly chosen gear ratios (30, 50, 75, 100 and a 115mph) and an urgent though restrained exhaust note not only to get you there and back in a hurry, but also to remind you now and then just how much enjoyment it is providing.

'Alfa steering is an acquired taste; absolutely dead of feel, yet able imperceptibly to transmit the most intimate information to your brain rather than to your body about what is going on

beneath the wheels, it annoys by its unwarranted heaviness at parking speeds far less than it delights by its lightness on the move, by its total freedom from tremor or hypersensitive vibration and most of all by the myriad proofs of its uncanny accuracy that somehow penetrate its

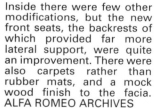

Inside there were few other modifications, but the new front seats, the backrests of which provided far more lateral support, were quite an improvement. There were also carpets rather than rubber mats, and a mock wood finish to the facia. ALFA ROMEO ARCHIVES

From the rear the GTV was distinguished by the Veloce script on the rear panel and a pair of rather beautiful enamel four-leafed clovers in ivory and green at the base of the rear pillars. The GTV's extra power made the car far more convincing as a Grand Tourer – a miniature Ferrari or Maserati. ALFA ROMEO ARCHIVES

The GTV featured the same instruments as the standard GT except that they were sunk into a wood-effect facia. The panel was well stocked – besides the usual instruments there were oil pressure and temperature gauges. Note the three unmarked toggle switches (ergonomics was a nascent art in those days) and the tachometer red-lined at 6,250rpm – as the twin cam's size increased, so its rev limit decreased.

superficial torpor.

'The same with the brakes; they too are short of feel, yet so well balanced that despite servo you can almost tell the precise moment when pad touches disc. The gearchange strikes a happy medium between insulation and mechanical precision, with vast but controlled sweeps of the long lever between ratios and a wonderfully firm spring-loading that makes of the often-difficult transfer from fourth to fifth speed a subconscious exertion rather than a physical battle.

'Yet there are shortcomings. We found no cause for complaint about the ride on normal British surfaces, but choppy lanes brought an irritating pitching motion, there was much roll on corners and any attempt at abandon on a humpback bridge would bring forth a jarring crunch from the region of that splendid, befinned sump.

'High-speed cruising on motorways was a noisy business, not so much for mechanical reasons (the engine is cheerful in its work, no more) as because the body generates at least three varieties of wind noise from each of its protuberances – most of all from the pillarless join between the windows and rear quarter-lights. As for roadholding, the saloon's sharp and sustained understeer gives way in the more compact coupe to a final flick of the other thing that can be put to good advantage by

Another view of the GTV's cabin, revealing the amazing degree of wraparound of the seat backrests. The backrests recline, though the knurled knobs that tilt them work in the opposite sense to that of most cars, a quirk that survives in today's Spider. Note the angle of the gear-lever, which provided a clean, if long-throw shift that was for many years a standard-setter.

locking the car hard over well before a sharp turn and letting it straighten under power on the way through . . . in the dry anyway; wet roads and regulation old-mix Cinturatos agree to differ amicably but early.

'Perhaps the significant thing is that the GTV, basically a five-year-old design, should be so much fun in its essentials and such good value', concluded *CAR*. So, plenty of enthusiasm for a machine that really seemed to gel in this latest development.

Not all was well at Casa Portello, though. As Alfa's production expanded rapidly to meet demand from its new customers, tales of poor quality and component failures began to gather momentum as it became apparent that the Giulia series had been developed a little too hastily. Stories of complete brake failure, snapped clutch cables and worn gearbox synchromesh were common, and so was evidence of poor paint and trim quality. And the owners, not surprisingly, were not happy.

These difficulties were not a total shock. Alfa Romeo was a fledgling mass manufacturer compared with Fiat and Ford, and sat on one of the steeper segments of the learning curve. Now it was being taught the painful way about thorough development, quality control and attention to detail. The growing ills were compounded by the cramped facilities at Portello, facilities and conditions which were no longer conducive to high quality.

A good job, then, that the shift to the expansive Arese plant coincided with the growth of the Giulia family. At least there was scope to introduce improvements here, and these were witnessed by *CAR Magazine* in late 1967 when its writers visited the Alfa factory. There they saw the range of checks performed during and after assembly, that every engine received a three-hour bench test and every car spent 15 minutes on a rolling road, followed by three laps of a demanding test circuit and a brake test. 'And finally', they wrote, 'we were delighted to note that the general blitz on trim standards and quality control has now extended to dip-painting and hand-rubbing down between coats for all bodies, a complete interior redesign for all saloon models and (as a detail example) replacement of the old rust-prone chrome bumpers with stainless steel on the complete coupe range – all this in addition to the revised braking system and completely redesigned gearbox synchro mechanism which were introduced as emergency measures at the time.' So, Alfa was at least learning something about development, and even if we now know that its measures to protect bodywork could have been more complete, the mechanicals have subsequently gained a reputation for being both robust and long-lived.

After what must have been a substantial investment in the coupe to order to improve its quality, few would have guessed at this stage that it was so far from its ultimate form and that it would have so much production life left in it. But that's a mark of sound design. The next stage of its evolution would come in tandem with similar changes made to the Spider, changes that would do much to cement these cars' reputations as pedigree high-performance machines.

The Veloce version of the Sprint GT did much to get the car established after its slow start, the combination of extra performance contributing to an upturn in sales. ALFA ROMEO ARCHIVES

CHAPTER 7

Major surgery

During the period when various developments were applied to the Sprint GT, little happened to alter the Spider, at least physically. However, its reputation received a huge boost at the hands of Dustin Hoffman, who drove a red Duetto, sometimes rather carelessly, in the 1967 film *The Graduate*. This exposure was most fortuitous because the Spider was not the first choice of car for Hoffman. The original plan had called for a more obvious sportscar of the era, such as an MG, but then a member of the film's crew saw a Duetto and suggested that the Alfa should be used instead. Hoffman's freedom machine is thought to survive to this day, having been converted into a racer for the American SCCA series.

Alfa salesmen in Britain talk of interest in the Spider receiving a boost whenever *The Graduate* is shown on television, and in the USA the cheapest Spider one can buy is named after the film.

Such massive publicity, though, did little to help sales at the time. In its best year the old Giulietta Spider managed a sales peak of 5,096 in 1960, a figure far beyond the reach of the new car during the 1960s. In 1966, the year of its launch, 3,363 Duettos went to new homes, and the following year the figure swelled only slightly to 3,812. The market simply didn't like the new car as much as the old one.

Fortunately, changes were on the way, and they were introduced remarkably soon after the car's launch. The first were seen at the Brussels show in January 1968 and they affected the entire Giulia range of saloon, coupe and Spider, the main alteration being a bigger engine, the twin-cam being enlarged to 1,779cc.

The new range was dubbed 1750 because Alfa wanted to cash in on some history. Otherwise, like any other manufacturer, it would have labelled the engine an 1800. Since the prewar sports models were amongst the most famous and highly regarded Alfas (though, ironically, they didn't sell well at the time) it was decided to use some heritage to push the new cars. You could call it a rather cynical manoeuvre, but the fact that there was little criticism of the badging at the time gives an idea of how well regarded the new cars became.

With the new engine came a fresh body for the Giulia range, the bigger Berlina saloon taking the line-up decisively upmarket. The Giulia saloon remained in production in various 1300 and 1600 guises while the new 1750 was intended to take on the larger-capacity BMW saloons that were nibbling their way into Alfa's territory.

The Berlina was a clever, if slightly ungainly adaptation of the Giulia saloon, Bertone managing to create a larger and more imposing machine out of hardware that was largely unchanged. Apart from the larger engine, the running gear was fundamentally similar to that of the Giulia saloon, modifications to the suspension consisting of nothing more than revised spring rates and the addition of a rear anti-roll bar, for example. That meant that the front and rear track remained unchanged, but the wheelbase was increased by almost 2in. The car's overall length grew significantly, though, providing a huge boot and more room around the engine, as well as slightly more lounging space. Like many Alfa saloons, the Berlina could hardly be called beautiful, but many found it easier on the eye than its smaller brother, and that fact, coupled with the name and the car's

The 1750 Berlina, a bigger saloon that supplemented the original Giulia saloon and was heavily based on it, took the range further upmarket where it competed more effectively against BMW. The Berlina was styled by Marcello Gandini, though he is better known for his Lamborghini Countach and Diablo. ALFA ROMEO ARCHIVES

The Berlina's cabin was more luxurious than the Giulia saloon's, a trend that the Spider and GTV would also take up. The interior was noticeably roomier than the Giulia's thanks to an extra 2in on the wheelbase. The track running gear remained the same as the smaller saloon's. ALFA ROMEO ARCHIVES

overall refinement, ensured it a reasonable market.

Having engineered a larger and more potent engine, it obviously made sense to install it in the performance models of the range, and so the 1750 Spider Veloce and 1750 GTV Coupe were launched simultaneously with the new saloon. The facelift also coincided with the need for more serious modifications to meet the needs of the American market. The 1750s used SPICA fuel injection to meet emissions regulations, side marker lamps were fitted and there were many other minor differences. Details of these, and all the other US variations, can be found in Appendix A.

Apart from a new engine and a new name (which allowed Alfa to drop the unsuccessful Duetto tag), the Spider barely changed at all, retaining the boat-tail style of the original design. There were a few detail changes, the most visible being a different design of road wheel, the original 15in rims being ditched in favour of more fashionable 5.5Jx14in items, which were an inch wider than previously. Fatter 165-14 tyres came with the new rims. A rear anti-roll bar was added and there were changes to the front suspension, the coils being softened and the wishbone geometry altered to raise the roll-centre and so

Though considerably more powerful than the Duetto, the 1750 Spider (the Duetto appellation was dropped) looked virtually identical, the main and subtle distinguishing feature being the fitment of 14in rather than 15in wheels. Power rose from 109bhp to 122bhp, and there was plenty more torque. There were also minor modifications to the suspension geometry and the brakes. ALFA ROMEO ARCHIVES

American regulations were having an impact by now, this Spider featuring the orange marker lights on the wings mandated by law. It also gained vestigial extra bumpers. The 1750 featured Spica mechanical fuel injection, necessary to meet the emissions regulations. ALFA ROMEO ARCHIVES

reduce lean during cornering. The brakes also gained the sophistication of a pressure-limiting valve for the rear axle, and the rotors were enlarged slightly.

There were minor changes in the cabin, including the appearance of a beautifully finished wood and aluminium three-spoke steering wheel, a revised ashtray, a leathercloth shroud to cover the convoluted rubber boot at the base of the gearlever, and the use of a less shiny vinyl for the seats. The fan switch had been moved from its distant location on the far side of the radio slot to a more convenient home closer to the instrument binnacle.

The changes to the engine involved widening the bores by 2mm and increasing the stroke by 6.5mm, which gave the dimensions of a rather old-fashioned unit. The block was stiffened and

the dynamo was dropped in favour of an alternator. The resulting inputs were modern enough, though, power climbing from the old 1600's 109bhp to 122bhp, delivered at 5,500rpm. Torque also grew, as might be expected of a larger-capacity, longer-stroke unit. Whereas the 1600 produced 103lb/ft of torque at 2,800rpm, the 1750 could muster 127lb/ft at 2,900rpm. More to the point, the torque curve was flatter right through the rev range, producing a more muscular performance.

So when *Motor* tested a 1750 boat-tail Spider in 1969 it discovered a decidedly brisker beast, capable of hitting 60mph in just 9.2sec and reaching a (hood-up) maximum of 116.4mph. That compared well with the 11.2sec and 111.1mph the same magazine managed with the original Duetto

The 1750 GTV was easier to distinguish from the 1600 version, having received a modest facelift to complement the extra power. Most obvious was the redesigned nose that did away with the stepped front panel, the bonnet now lying flush with it. There were four headlamps – the inners were main beam-only driving lamps – a new and very attractive grille and indicator/sidelight units mounted on the front bumper.
ALFA ROMEO ARCHIVES

1600. The 1750 also pulled more strongly, recording a 7.0sec 40–60mph time in fourth (8.2sec for the Duetto) and 10.9sec for the same increment in fifth as against 12.4sec in the old car.

This is what the test team thought of the car's performance: 'With the extra capacity of the larger engine came an inevitable increase in power, but the designers really concentrated on torque; the way it can pull from under 20mph in fifth gear with just a little throttle feeding is as impressive as it is academic for an Alfa driver – it is slow but there is only slight judder at 1,400rpm or so. What is more practical is that for most town driving you can stay quietly in third and there is ample torque to pull away from right-angle street turns at 10–15mph. At the other end of the scale it pulls smoothly and lustily all the way to the red, which starts at 6,200rpm; we used 7,000rpm in our acceleration tests, clearing 60mph in second gear

after only 9.2 seconds from rest. Most of the time on the road one never goes beyond 5,000rpm because there is a gear for every occasion.'

Of the chassis modifications the testers had this to say: 'That we were happy to take the car round MIRA at that speed (about 115mph) reflects our confidence in its suspension and general roadholding behaviour. Its steering is a little heavy and springy, but the wheel is well placed to get the wrists cocked for full effort; it transmits a particularly good wet road feel, is direct without the low-geared feeling of the Alfa saloons and is free of kick-back. On dry roads grip is very good and the final oversteer is controllable and easy to use to tighten the line, but the rear anti-roll bar is really too stiff as the inside wheel lifts very easily in slow corners to give wheelspin under power. One needs to be cautious on wet roads.' Despite this and a few other reservations, *Motor* reckoned 'in detail it is not perfect but in total concept it comes near to it'.

Other magazines were more emphatic about the improvements to the Spider's handling, *Road & Track* commenting: 'The rear anti-roll bar, which was a new item for the 1750 series, reduced the traditional Alfa Romeo understeer. Directional stability is very good and the car is easily kept in line or manoeuvred at all speeds. As speeds increase there is a gradual transition from understeer to oversteer. This is in keeping with the nature of the car, the car not moving out until it is at maximum cornering speed for prevailing conditions. The car can be cornered cleanly by anyone; those skillful enough to deserve a car like this can vary the attitude with more power. Stability for the prudent, sport for the enthusiastic.'

Motor magazine were at least as enthusiastic about the 1750 GTV: 'A flat spot at around 2,000rpm (probably peculiar to the test car) and a tendency for the inside rear wheel to lift and spin were the only minor criticisms we could find in what many of our test staff came to regard as their ideal car.'

The GTV, weighing much the same as the Spider, showed similarly improved zest. There were other changes to go with the new engine, including smaller-diameter, wider wheels, altered front suspension geometry, a rear anti-roll bar and upgraded brakes, as well as a fairly major facelift. The changes were designed by Alfa's own styling department, Giugiaro and Bertone having had no further involvement in the car's design after its launch.

The most obvious alterations were to the nose.

The 1750 GTV rode on 14in wheels rather than the 15in variety previously worn by the coupe, and enjoyed a number of modifications to the suspension. Detail mods visible here include the deletion of the rectangular side repeaters, new hubcaps and a new roundel at the base of the rear pillars; the quadrifoglio was finished in gold on an ivory background. ALFA ROMEO ARCHIVES

There was minimal change at the rear of the car, the chief difference being the addition of an Alfa badge and below it the 1750 script. Note the crude location of the reversing lamp below the rear bumper, a feature of all the early cars. ALFA ROMEO ARCHIVES

The front panel was realigned so that it sat flush with the bonnet, there were now four headlamps, the inner pair being smaller 7in driving lights that lit with the main beams, and there was a new and very elegant grille. Other exterior changes included the deletion of the rectangular side repeater flashers, their job being taken over, at the front at least, by new wraparound indicators that sat (rather untidily) on top of the bumper, where they were more vulnerable to damage.

Detail changes ran to a gold-on-white quadrifoglio badge at the base of each rear pillar, and an Alfa roundel was planted over a fresh indent on the bootlid to supplement the new 1750 script. The hubcaps were also subtly changed. This was not a massive batch of modifications because this was not a shape that needed radical resculpting, but the fresh front end gave the car a more sophisticated and aggressive mien, making it seem more grown-up and mature.

The cabin was considerably more sophisticated, too, to match the increasingly grand aspirations of the affluent few who could afford pedigree sportscars. Most of the major kit was new, only the carpets and trim panels surviving the upgrade more or less unchanged. The facia was now dominated by a dramatically large speedo and tachometer that sat in pods visible through the top half of the wooden three-spoke steering wheel, which was also new. The rev-counter was angled so that the red sector came at the top of the dial, closest to the driver's line of sight, and it also housed the oil pressure gauge. Like the tacho, the speedometer was marked so that higher velocities came close to the base of the screen, and it housed warning lights for the alternator and

The 1750 GTV was given an all-new interior, probably the best of the series. Real wood replaced the Fablon variety, the major instruments were big and beautifully presented, the wheel was wood-rimmed with polished alloy spokes and there was now a full-length centre console into which more instruments, the heater controls and some switchgear were located. The seats were new, the front pair featuring flying-buttress side bolsters and the passenger chair (only) a retractable headrest. ALFA ROMEO ARCHIVES

blower motor.

Instead of Fablon fake wood there was now a strip of the real thing to give the dash a lift, a theme continued to the new centre console, which dropped steeply before curving at the forward edge of the seats to run the full length of the transmission tunnel. The console housed circular dials, angled towards the driver, for water temperature and fuel tank contents. The gearlever sprouted from a PVC boot below, the heater slides mounted to one side of it (the wrong one for RHD), and beneath that were three tab switches for the dual-speed wipers, the panel lights and the two-speed fan.

Hand throttle and choke were still hung to one side of the steering column and illuminated (rather too brightly) at night. On the other side of the column was a cigar lighter which was unusual in that you pushed the cigar or cigarette into it for ignition. Behind this was a rotary knob for zeroing the trip meter, and on the floor to the left of the clutch was the washer pump plunger which also triggered the wipers, but never for long enough to sweep the screen clean. Buried near this was the relocated fuse box, which was previously on the offside inner wing under the bonnet, where it was rather susceptible to damp, dirt and the odd dropped spanner. The 1750 Spider also benefited from this modification. Italian cars had a reputation for duff electrics by this time, and this was clearly a minor bid to fix the problem.

If the bold new instruments were dramatic, the

front seats were even more so. For a start they didn't match, the passenger's incorporating a headrest that could be extended, rather laboriously, by twirling a winged knob. Both seats featured flying buttress side bolsters, the idea being that the gap between these and the backrest would improve airflow around a hot and bothered occupant's back. The cushions were heavily ribbed to the same end.

A curious modification was the change of headlining, which was brought about by the FIA's racing rules. These required that the GTV qualify as a saloon, meaning that it should offer a certain minimum rear cabin space, and in order to meet it the GTV's ceiling had to be raised, which is why there is a padded recessed insert in the headlining over the rear seats on later models.

The interior redesign was very effective, giving the car a much classier, finished air. Of all the Giulia GT interiors, this one ranks as the best stylistically. Unfortunately, it also happens to be the most fragile, but more of that later.

The 1750 GTV was very well received, the extra power making for a more exciting drive without in any way upsetting the car's balance. That was always a risk because the Giulia's chassis design was simply a development of the Giulietta's, a car originally engineered for a 1300 motor of relatively modest output. That basically the same chassis could accommodate a 1.8-litre engine without being embarrassed was a measure of the soundness of the design.

The 1750 GTV did much to bolster sales of the

Sprint, which was soon to become decisively more popular. In the first full year of sales Alfa shifted almost 11,000 Sprint GTs, and the figure hovered at much the same level for the next couple of seasons. But what really got the volume swelling was the introduction of the 1300 GT Junior, which helped sales to virtually double. The reason was Italy's longstanding fondness for cars of small engine capacity, largely brought about by fiscal measures which penalize cars of over 1,600cc.

The Junior appeared in September 1966 in the original step-front bodyshell and with the original running gear, and it was not updated with the 14in wheels and the other changes that came with the 1750 until the beginning of 1969. It was essentially the same as the Sprint GT, but with less luxury. For example, there were rubber mats instead of carpets, an all-plastic three-spoke steering wheel, cheaper hubcaps and a simplified grille which had a single chrome bar spanning the black mesh between the Alfa shield and the lamps and indicators. The front seats were not as sporting, either, their backrests being less bolstered.

The Junior was not a desperately powerful beast, mustering some 89bhp at 6,000rpm, which nevertheless was not a bad output for a 1300 of the day. Also, the mechanicals were just as sophisticated, with twin Weber carburettors, twin camshafts, a five-speed gearbox and disc brakes all round, and further compensation was to be found in the engine's zest for revs, 7,000rpm

being easily, if rather pointlessly, within reach.

If the GT-J was not exactly a road rocket, it nevertheless won over drivers because it made such a nice package. Road tests of the day certainly didn't condemn it for sloth, and here, for example, is *Cars and Car Conversions*' verdict: 'There is not a lot of low-speed torque and the power starts to happen at about two-five, but with five near-perfectly spaced gear ratios at your command, who the hell cares about torque? The great thing about the Alfa is that it has to be driven all the time, and This Is Fun, to put it mildly. You can thrash about the countryside to your heart's content, even in these benighted, restricted days, using the gearlever to chase the rev-counter needle up and down the dial; try it on quiet but interesting country lanes to get the maximum effect – particularly if you happen to be motoring in East Anglia at sugar-beet time, when the roads tend to accumulate a nice layer of slime!'

The 1300 GT Junior was joined by a small-engined Spider in June 1968, the 1600 having been replaced by the 1750. The Spider 1300 Junior was mechanically identical to the GT-J, but it did nothing like as much to bolster interest in the model, sales of which at the time were dwindling. Instead, the 1300 merely formed the bulk of Spider sales, which must have reduced Alfa's profits somewhat. Trim differences between the Junior and the 1750 were small, the most obvious being the deletion of the Perspex fairings over the headlamps, but in addition there were repositioned side repeater flashers and simplified

The GT Junior was launched in 1966 with an 89bhp engine, a model that did much to boost sales of the car in Italy, where small engines are favoured. Though not particularly fast, the 1300 motor was very sweet, revving to 7,000rpm easily. It had rubber mats rather than carpets, a plastic three-spoke wheel, less bolstered front seats, a simpler grille and cheaper hubcaps. ALFA ROMEO ARCHIVES

The Spider 1300 Junior appeared in June 1968 looking more or less identical to the original Duetto, and continued in round-tail form after the Kamm-tail 1750 arrived in late 1970. ALFA ROMEO ARCHIVES

hubcaps for further exterior identification, besides the 1300 Junior script on the bootlid. Inside, the cigar lighter had gone and there was a two-spoke aluminium-and-plastic wheel in place of the wooden three-spoke version. Not much had been changed when you consider that the Junior was over 20% cheaper than the 1750 and must have cost virtually the same to manufacture.

None of which deterred Alfa from considering further changes to the Spider, which had its curvy rump sliced right off in November 1970. The change was drawn by Pininfarina's rather than Alfa's own design centre, and it accompanied a battery of other alterations which did much to update the Spider's appearance and, to many, turn it into more of an aesthetic success.

Removal of the round tail shortened the car noticeably, taking 6.2in off its length, an inevitable corollary of which was marginally reduced boot capacity, which fell from 7.5 to 6.9cu ft. But this was still more than some sportscars could offer. The Kamm tail (Dr Kamm was an aerodynamicist) improved the car's Cd, (however, no figures appear to be available, nor are there road tests of mechanically equivalent round-tail and Kamm-tail models to prove a higher top speed), and reduced its vulnerability to parking damage.

New, larger lamp clusters into which the designers had remembered to incorporate the reflectors as well as reversing lights, a cut-out in the valance for the exhaust, a more substantial rubber-faced rear bumper and a bold new badge script completed the rear-end freshening.

More subtle was the slightly more raked front screen, which now featured conventionally arranged wiper arms rather than the old, less effective, if more elegant clap-hands set-up. The side repeaters were moved to the forward edge of the front wings, and the door handles were changed for a pair of beautifully sculpted flush-fitting devices that have subsequently been used on several Ferraris.

The nose was altered slightly, too, though there were no sheet metal alterations. Instead, the Alfa shield was widened and the quarter-bumpers redesigned for a more integrated appearance; there were also more flush-fitting sidelight and indicator units.

The redesign inside was at least as far-reaching. The painted dash had gone, to be replaced by a modern, injection-moulded sculpture that looked vastly more luxurious. Set into this were some of the most voluptuous looking instrument nacelles yet seen in a car, which housed the speedometer and rev-counter. In the middle of the dash, in much the same place as they had been before, were the trio of supplementary gauges for fuel, oil pressure and water temperature, along with a quartet of warning lights. Beneath was a slot for the radio, and below that a full-length centre console, which was of much the same design as the GTV's with its heater slides and switches for wipers, panel lights and heater fan, except that it was in black plastic rather than wood. At the end of the console, behind the ashtray, were the repositioned choke and hand throttle knobs.

The face-level vents of the old car were carried over, as were the adjustable screen demister grilles and the door trim panels, though the door and window winder handles were redesigned. The seats were much the same except that they now had head restraints.

Mechanical changes were few, but worth knowing about. Most important was the change to dual-circuit brakes and, for left-hand-drive cars, a switch to pendant hinging for the brake and clutch pedals. Unfortunately, right-hand-drive cars stayed with the original floor-hinged set-up, which meant that the clutch and brake master cylinders were still slung beneath the floor where they were vulnerable to corrosion. A further

Late in 1970 the Spider had a major facelift at the hands of Filippo Sapino, later head of Ford's Ghia design house, but then an employee of Pininfarina. The big change was chopping off the rounded tail and giving the car an aerodynamic Kamm tail. Not that Sapino knew how aerodynamic it was. He says today: 'I was vaguely aware that it was beneficial, but we never tested the car to prove it.' ALFA ROMEO ARCHIVES

Sapino also increased the rake of the front windscreen and the degree of tumblehome – the amount the glass leans inwards – of the side glass. The bumpers were redesigned and the grille was squatter and lower, no longer necessitating the little lump in the nose of the early cars. There were also new rear lamps, the wipers were conventionally mounted rather than being the clap-hands type, and the door handles were replaced with beautiful flush-fit items. ALFA ROMEO ARCHIVES

The interior was also completely reworked. The facia was now completely moulded, and sunk into it were a pair of giant nacelles housing speedo and rev-counter. The minor gauges remained in their central location, but there was now a centre console housing the gear-lever, heater controls, some switchgear and an ashtray. The door trim panels were redesigned and the seats gained head restraints. ALFA ROMEO ARCHIVES

The GTV received a few detail changes at the same time as the Spider's facelift late in 1970, chief of which were matching seats that had wind-up head restraints and, optionally, the cloth trim shown here. ALFA ROMEO ARCHIVES

difference for RHD cars was the use of twin servo units, for reasons of under-bonnet packaging.

Changes were also made to the engine, which were carried across to the Berlina and to the 1750 GTV, which similarly received detail changes in 1970. The engine modifications were mostly designed to cure excessive piston slap. New pistons and liners were fitted, the pistons featuring offset gudgeon pins. They also operated at a lower compression, the ratio falling from 9.5 to 9.1:1, which accounts for the slightly lower power output of 118bhp generally quoted for the 1750 engine, rather than 122bhp.

Before this there had been changes to the air intake system, the air cleaner and its convoluted air intake tube that ran over the top of the engine having been changed for a simpler tubular filter box that clipped directly to the carburettors.

There were some detail alterations to the GTV as well. Left-hand-drive models received the same pendant clutch and brake pedal as the Spider, and there were dual-circuit brakes (twin servo units for RHD GTVs for the same reason as with the RHD Spiders) and quartz-iodine lights. There were new bumpers, which were squarer and more slender than before and this time fitted with overriders, and the front indicators were now let into the bodywork.

Inside, the wild-looking seats of the original car were replaced by more conventional-looking seats; there was now a matching pair in the front, with wind-up head restraints and without the flying buttress bolsters. They were less sporty,

but were probably more acceptable to the majority of customers.

This was the busiest period for the GTV in terms of modifications, and there would be one more round of alterations before the model would die, creating the fastest cars of the series, GTAs excluded. Alfa doubtless thought at the time that the parallel improvements carried out on the Spider would also be the last for that model, but in the early 1970s the little sportscar still had a long career ahead of it. Meanwhile, what came next was probably the optimum version.

CHAPTER 8

Maturity at last

Though the 1750s were successful cars, taking Alfa's production rate to over 100,000 for the first time in 1969, sales were not as strong as they might have been. After a year, in fact, they dropped a shade, suggesting that the strategy might not have been as clever as it had seemed.

The trouble was mainly on the domestic market, where the 1750s attracted much higher tax penalties for their relatively large engines, yet didn't really offer the performance advantages that 2-litre rivals such as the BMW 2000 provided. The climb to 1,779cc simply wasn't bold enough – a still bigger engine was needed to make the tax penalty worth paying.

It came in June 1971, two and a half years after the 1750s appeared. Not that you'd notice the difference, at least in the Spider's case, unless you drove it, because there were virtually no trim or styling changes to signal the move. All you were given was a 2000 badge instead of the 1750 script on the tail panel, and a new wheel and hubcap design.

But there's no doubt that the Spider went a lot harder, as might be expected when its power had climbed from 118 to 132bhp. But it was not the 2-litre motor's outright power that impressed so much as its torque, which had improved considerably. The peak showed only a modest gain, to 132lb/ft at 3,500rpm from 127lb/ft at 2,900rpm, but the torque curve was fatter, making the car considerably more relaxed to drive, strong acceleration being instantly available

The 2-litre Spider looked virtually identical to the 1750, being distinguished only by its badge and new hub covers. Power climbed to 132bhp from 118bhp. ALFA ROMEO ARCHIVES

in any gear from low engine speeds.

There was a downside, though, which was the engine's greater thirst (not unexpectedly) and its reduced enthusiasm for revs. The red line drew the curtains at just 5,700rpm now, and the motor just didn't sound as sweet as the 1750 at high crankshaft speeds. This, and its noticeably better fuel consumption, made the 1750 engine something of the enthusiasts' favourite among the twin-cams, though almost as many find the 2-litre's extra muscle hard to resist.

This is how the Australian magazine *Sports Car World* described the contrast: 'The difference between the two-litre Alfas and the old 1750s is that the 2000s immediately feel somehow more masculine. The engines are torquier from lower revs, feel more full-bellied – and this impression tends to filter right through the car.

'Where the 1750 engine was delightfully smooth and willing from 2,000rpm upwards, yet went decidedly harder once it reached 4,500, the two-litre feels much flatter, pulling hard from little more than 1,000rpm instead of 2,000 and having noticeably more strength in the 2,000 to 4,000 rev range. However, it doesn't appear to have quite the sparkle of the little engine above 4,000rpm, though it is, of course, still tremendously strong and smooth.

'For this reason it could perhaps be described as less of an endearing enthusiasts' engine because it doesn't feel to have quite the charm and character of the 1750 to someone who really loves highly-bred engines.

'But for everyday use the 2000 is preferable, for it is a lazier, lustier mill that's stronger away from the line and better suited to minimal gearchange in city snarls.'

The extra zest was less evident against the stopwatch because of the new motor's limited scope for revving compared with the old. The 9.2sec 0–60mph sprint recorded by *Motor* for the round-tail 1750 only fell to 8.8sec when *Autocar* tested a Kamm-tail 2000 (neither magazine tested both models) and the top speed didn't climb at all, remaining at 116mph, which was confirmation of the Spider's turbulent high-speed aerodynamics, a drawback shared with most ragtops.

The biggest improvement came with the in-gear times, where the torque was at its most telling. The 30–50mph span in fourth fell from 7.6sec to 6.4sec, which is rapid even today, and there were similar shortenings over other bands and in other gears. It made the Spider a great overtaker.

The engine's capacity increase came about by widening the bore from 80 to 84mm, taking it from 1,779 to 1,962cc. Since there was only limited metal left in a block that had started out as a 1300, the bore change was achieved in part by slightly re-arranging the liner centres. Otherwise, there were virtually no changes other than that the oil filter was now of the spin-on canister type. The valve diameters and cam profiles remained the same, as did the compression ratio, carburation and, for that matter, the gearing.

The only other technical nicety to arrive – and it was a useful one – was the option of a mechanical limited-slip differential, which was usually fitted to UK-specification cars. It did much to reduce the inside wheel's habit of lifting and spinning.

The GTV changed more visibly, though, gaining a whole series of detail changes besides the new mechanical package. Most obvious was yet another front grille treatment, this time a series of horizontal chrome bars into which the Alfa shield was sculpted to stand proud. The new grille was certainly simpler to manufacture and attach to the car, but there is no doubt that it had lost the elegance of the 1750's treatment. Other modifications included reprofiled rear wheelarches, allowing bulkier rubber to be fitted (though Alfa didn't provide it), the standardization of a heated rear window and a redesign for the rear lamp clusters, which were widened to accommodate reversing lamps. The GTV also gained the new steel wheels and stainless steel hub centres fitted to the Spider, and the quadrifoglio badge at the base of the rear

pillars was swapped for a cheaper roundel featuring a green Alfa serpent.

But the biggest alteration was to the interior, where yet another new dashboard was to be found. It was an improvement in some respects, a major gain being the addition of a pair of very effective eyeball face-level vents at each end, besides the regrouping of the instruments so that they appeared in a single cluster. Sadly, though, the new dials had lost much of the elegance of the giant-sized speedo and tachometer of the 1750s. They were smaller, less clearly marked, no longer angled so that the most important portions were easiest to read and, strangely, had blue faces, which if nothing else made them distinctive.

The oil pressure gauge sat in the base of the rev-counter while the separate fuel and temperature gauges snuggled between the two main dials. Beneath them were two batches of warning lights enclosed in two quartered circles, intended to mimic four-leaved clovers. It was intriguing, but contrived.

Now that it no longer housed any dials, the centre console was less steeply sloped at its front end in order to accommodate an optional air

The Spider still looked good with its hood up, which is not always the case with a convertible. The hood was remarkably easy to raise and lower, setting a standard in this respect which is maintained even today. The only drawbacks were poor rear three-quarter visibility, and occasional leaks, the bane of many a soft-top. ALFA ROMEO ARCHIVES

conditioning system, and it no longer ran all the way to the base of the back seat. The twin column stalks remained as before, despite the fact that the wipers should have been triggered by one, and the choke and hand throttle controls held station to one side of the steering column. The wooden wheel had changed, its trio of horn pushes shortened and the boss now made of plastic rather than wood. The rest of the cabin, including the seats, was much the same, though cloth was now available. Further luxury options now included electric front windows (of dubious value when they're Italian) and the air conditioning previously mentioned.

Despite the fact that it was a new version of a relatively old car, there was still plenty of enthusiasm for the GTV in the press. *Autocar* summed up a 2000 GTV tested in 1972 like this: 'With the 2000 engine, the GTV moves into the performance class many customers expect of it; it is now a genuinely quick car with relaxed 100–110mph cruising capability. Alfa's efforts of recent years to improve detail and overall finish show to advantage; the car is a really attractive package for those prepared to spend the extra for a pretty GTV body rather than the angular saloon. As always, the real attraction of the car is its feeling of precision and responsiveness; the extra power seems to have added to this without detracting from anything.'

CAR Magazine had much that was good to say about the 2000 GTV, particularly of its handling, which stacked up well in a giant test against an Audi 100 Coupe (remember those?) and the BMW 2002 Tii in November 1972. 'The spontaneous impression that one gets from the Alfa is of refinement. And never does the car make you change your mind. It has a lot of roadholding, of course, and the handling is exceptionally good by any standard, certainly superior to that of the Audi or the BMW. At 3.6 turns lock to lock, the steering is lower geared than this figure would suggest because the turning circle verges on 40 feet when you go left and 36 feet or so on the opposite lock. But where it scores is in responsiveness without twitch. It really does encourage the driver to behave in a precise way and the handling answers exactly as it should. We found ourselves belting hard and just edging the tail outwards a couple of degrees to hurry the GTV on its way through twisty country; never did it give the feeling that we were getting to the ragged edge and that to transgress it would break down communications.'

Motor was keen, too, but like *CAR*, found a bit to criticize. The positives were pretty gushing, though: '. . . evolutionary refinement . . . has transformed the Alfa coupe over the years from a rather stark and fragile fun car into the compact executive's express it is today. That such refinement has been achieved while amplifying, not sacrificing, those qualities that make it so enjoyable to drive is surely the root of the GTV's success. It's certainly why we still rate it among our favourites.'

Specific plus points included an engine that

The Berlina 2000 looked much the same as the 1750, changes being restricted to the grille, which was now largely matt black, and the hubcaps. CAR MAGAZINE

The Berlina's cabin was revised more extensively and featured new instruments with white faces, a different steering wheel and assorted detail improvements, including an air conditioning option, which was also available on the GTV. ALFA ROMEO ARCHIVES

The GTV changed rather more than the Spider when it received the 2000 engine, this shot showing the new grille with its horizontal chrome bars. It is considered less elegant than the 1750 grille, and lasts only a few months before pimples of corrosion appear. The bumper and sidelight/indicator units were unchanged from the Mark 2 version of the 1750. CAR MAGAZINE

'pulls with considerable vigour from about 2,000rpm', 'a superb five-speed gearbox', and the testers liked the limited-slip diff, finding 'no trouble getting the power on to the road in mid-corner', which meant that 'the Alfa could be cornered very rapidly indeed without getting out of line. When you add up all these assets – the vigorous performance assisted by five perfect gear ratios, the high cornering powers allied to the

The cabin of the GTV was extensively altered from the 1750's, there being a new dash and centre console – to accommodate an air conditioning unit – and door trims. The console no longer ran the full length of the transmission tunnel, and there were very effective eyeball vents in the dash. There were no modifications to the switchgear, though. The seats remained unchanged – sensibly, given that they had been highly praised by orthopaedic specialists – continuing to be offered in either cloth or vinyl. Occasionally, cars were leather-trimmed. CAR MAGAZINE

The 2000 GTV's new instruments were not as classical as the 1750's, though all were now located immediately in front of the driver and, strangely, finished in blue. The cloverleaf shapes below the fuel and temperature gauges incorporated the warning lights. The wheel boss was now plastic rather than wood. Just below the wheel's left spoke can be seen the controls for choke and hand throttle. ALFA ROMEO ARCHIVES

From the rear, the main change was to the lamp clusters, which were enlarged to incorporate reversing lamps. There was new script for the boot badge, and the rear wheelarch profile was raised to accommodate fatter tyres which the factory never actually offered. CAR MAGAZINE

From the side, the 2000 was virtually indistinguishable from the 1750, the reprofiled rear arches, new hubcaps and altered roundel at the base of the rear pillars – it featured a green serpent rather than the gold cloverleaf – being the only identification points. CAR MAGAZINE

handy size – it's easy to understand why the 2000 GTV makes such short (and entertaining) work of cross country journeys'.

Complaints were mounting, though, as you would expect of what was now quite an old car. The writers attacked 'the small boot and cramped rear quarters', 'wind noise from the front quarter-lights', the GTV's thirst (20.8mpg – 'on the heavy side'), 'a firm ride – rather jittery over secondary surfaces but seldom harsh or crashy – indicating that some resilience has been sacrificed in the interests of handling', and the pedals – 'our biggest gripe'. The GTV also collected black marks for its driving position and switchgear. Overall, though, the magazine reckoned 'the Alfa bears its years remarkably well'.

Just as well, because its career was far from over in 1972, with another five years to run before the final 1600 GT Junior was sold in Britain. The Junior always trailed the GTVs when it came to picking up improvements, and it managed to live the longest, slotting beneath the relatively fresh Alfetta GT at the end.

The 1300 first gained a brake servo and two-speed wipers in 1968, then the hydraulically triggered clutch, 14in road wheels, extra sound-proofing, the rear brake pressure limiting valve and the suspension mods, including a rear anti-roll bar, in January 1969, over a year after these changes were featured on the GTV. And it didn't

get the new dashboard and flush-fitting bonnet until early 1971, when a 1600 GT Junior was introduced to fill the gap between the 2000 GTV and the 1300 GT-J.

The facelifted Juniors had single headlamps rather than the twins of the GTV, they used the original rear lamp clusters, did without overriders and badging at the base of the rear pillars, and were rather spartan inside. They also had the dashboard that came with the 1750s, with its massive main dials, the wood trimmings and a wood-rimmed steering wheel, but the seats were simpler, rubber matting covered the floor, and there was no centre console.

This meant that the supplementary gauges hung rather untidily behind the gearlever, below the heater slides, and that the switches for wipers, fan and panel lights were screwed into the facia, along with sundry warning lights. The changes were not numerous, perhaps, but they certainly contrived to make the Junior a considerably less opulent looking machine than the GTV.

Nevertheless, the GTV was fun to drive, even in 1300 form, as CAR Magazine discovered in September 1971 in a comparison with the Fiat 124 1600 Coupe. The Alfa was not desperately quick (12.7sec for 0–60mph and 104mph) and was certainly slower than the Fiat, but the testers found its engine more enjoyable, explaining: 'The factory engine people have a gift for endowing each Alfa four-cylinder with a taut, almost twangy feel of urgency. Undoubtedly that burpy exhaust note helps, but the sensation is more physical, less aural, than that. We've revelled in it in bigger Alfas in the past and found it just as pronounced in the 1300.

'Like the Fiat, the Alfa gains a lot of its ability from being very generously carburettored. It pays to keep the revs high, although there is adequate torque from mid-range speeds. A snap throttle opening at very low revs reveals a big flat spot on the Fiat, while the Alfa can actually splutter away to a stall unless you catch it.' As you would expect, the testers found this 1300 GT Junior much the same as the more pricey Bertone coupes in other departments (which meant good and entertaining, but flawed in a number of details), and in this comparison that was enough to give it the edge over the Fiat.

The same engine appeared in the 1300 Junior Spider, and this model, like the Junior coupe,

received its updates later than the bigger-engined models. The Kamm tail treatment came in 1970, along with all the other exterior detail changes, but the interior remained as for the original Duetto, with the painted metal facia and cheaper fittings. A 1600 Junior joined the smaller-engined model in 1972.

The 1600 engine fitted to the GT and Spider Juniors was virtually the same as the 109bhp unit fitted to the original step-front GT Veloce, gaining just 1bhp to make the output 110, while the 1300 motor remained unchanged at 89bhp, which was just about enough to provide some excitement.

For the GT Junior there was a final bit of catching up in June 1974 when it gained the 2000 GTV bodyshell, with its revised rear arches, and the interior from the same car, with virtually all the same luxury appointments. Apart from the engine the two models were identical mechanically, although the limited-slip differential was not

The GT Junior gained the improvements afforded the GTV later in the day. This is a 1971 1300 GT-J, featuring the flush bonnet, revised indicators and the twin instrument pod facia of the 1750, prior to having 14in wheels, revised suspension and upgraded brakes. The 1971 improvements coincided with the introduction of the 1600 GT-J. ALFA ROMEO ARCHIVES

The GT Junior interior of 1971 to 1974 was considerably cheaper-looking than the 1750's despite the sharing of the same main dashboard architecture. The Junior did without a centre console, the minor instruments being crudely hung below the heater controls, while rubber and plastic mats covered the floor and the seats were less elaborate. Note the choke and hand throttle, located under the steering column. ALFA ROMEO ARCHIVES

Despite the single headlamps and lack of overriders, the Junior still looked classy. Note the different hub covers from those of the earlier Junior. ALFA ROMEO OWNERS CLUB

available with the Junior, even as an option. By this time only the 1600 GT-J was available in Britain, the 1300 having disappeared early in the Seventies.

Production of the coupe finished in 1976, by which time its replacement, the Alfetta GT, had been on sale for two years, continuing Alfa's policy of offering both old and new coupes simultaneously for a while. The two versions of the old car were offered unchanged to the end, the last Juniors being sold in 1977. However, there was a limited-edition version of the 2000, the SE, that came close to the end of the model's life. It is not known how many of these were built, Alfa's records having been lost when the UK concession

The Spider Junior was offered as a 1300 and, from 1972, a 1600, the Kamm-tail body being adopted from 1970, but with the original painted dashboard. This shot shows a late Junior with more modern seats and carpeting, a version that did not reach the UK. ALFA ROMEO ARCHIVES

was sold to TKM in the late Eighties, but there were probably a few hundred of them.

Surprisingly, the specification of SEs varied considerably, but all were given a vinyl roof in either black or tobacco (which was actually nailed into position under the front and rear screen seals), a set of Campanatura alloy wheels, tinted glass and a double coach tape along the flanks. The wiper arms, door mirror, grille and headlamp bezels were finished in matt black, which was a rather pathetic bid to make the car look more modern than it actually was. A roof-mounted aerial and rear parcel shelf-mounted speakers were also standard, along with either a radio or a radio-cassette player, and there was a pair of rear fog-guard lamps. Some models also came with electric windows, leather trim and a fabric Webasto sunroof. How many of each specification were built will almost certainly remain a mystery, not least because it was probably as dependent on the parts in stock at the time of build as on what the UK market actually ordered.

When production of the Bertone coupe finally ended, 210,495 had been built during the 13-year production run. The most numerous of these were 1300 Juniors, though few of the 91,964 cars built went into the UK market, the majority remaining in Italy, a market which, as previously explained, favoured small-engined machinery. There were 44,276 1750s and 37,921 2000 GTVs, proving that the GTV had remarkable staying

power during its long life, which rather underscores the enduring beauty of its lines and the farsightedness of its mechanical design.

These may not be massive volumes by the standards of today, but they were quite high numbers for a specialty coupe at a time when the world car market was considerably smaller than it was destined to become. The GTV must have done more than almost any other Alfa to publicize the brand and ram home the idea that Alfa build glamorous, sporty and affordable cars.

The Spider helped, of course, but it was never made in anything approaching the quantities of the coupe and, in Europe at least, it was a much rarer sight. Its development continued in a rather desultory way, Alfa simply playing games with engines to suit various markets. Money was spent on it reluctantly, not least because the slow build rate meant a slow payback. It was only in the Eighties that Alfa began to realize that if it didn't have immortality on its side, the Spider had something approaching it, and began investing again.

In the meantime, the arrival of the 2000 version prompted Alfa to reintroduce the 1600 engine in 1972, now that there was such a big gap between the 1300 Junior and the 2000. Essentially, the 1600 motor was offered as an option on the 1300 Junior, the cars being otherwise similar in every respect. The engine was the same 110bhp unit found in the GT Junior, though it was detuned to

Externally, the Spider Junior looked much the same as the 2000, except for the deletion of the Perspex headlamp fairings and the retention of the old door handles. ALFA ROMEO ARCHIVES

102bhp for rationalization reasons in 1974, Alfa standardizing on this version of the 1600 engine, which was used in the high-volume Giulia Super.

The two Spider Juniors used the same Kamm-tail bodyshell as the 2000, the 1300 having been upgraded in 1970, but the interior was more or less as for the original Duetto, featuring the painted steel dash and separate main instrument binnacle. One of the few differences was the use of a wood-rimmed three-spoke steering wheel in place of the original black plastic wheel. The pair were offered unchanged until 1974, when they received the same interior treatment as the more expensive 2000s.

In 1975 the 2000 was slightly detuned for reasons of production rationalization, though not as severely as the 1600 had been, peak power falling off from 132bhp at 5,500rpm to 128bhp at 5,300rpm. Torque also dropped off slightly, falling from 137lb/ft at 3,500rpm to 132lb/ft at 4,300rpm, and the engine continued in this tune,

in European markets at least, until 1982.

It was during this period that exports to Britain came to an end. The 1300 and 1600 Juniors had been imported in facelifted form, with the Kamm tail and painted dashboard, but never with the revised dash. This left just the 2000 Veloce, imports of which continued until 1978, by which time Type Approval differences between the UK and other European markets, plus the mechanical complexities of right-hand drive, made it increasingly inconvenient to continue offering the car in Britain, where sales in any case were small. So it disappeared from the UK price lists in September 1978 after a 12-year run.

Alfa must have reckoned on the model dying relatively soon anyway, though its original plan for a replacement in the form of a targa-topped Alfetta Spider had long been abandoned. Few people could have guessed at that time that the Spider was destined for three facelifts and would live for more than a quarter of a century.

CHAPTER 9

Coupe dies, Spider thrives

Perhaps the best proof that the Spider's style was ahead of its time can be found among the sales records. Things did not go well in the early days, the Duetto achieving nowhere near the sales of its predecessor, which regularly turned in annual figures in excess of 5,000. After peaking in 1967 at 3,812 units, Spider sales declined until 1972, when the 2000 version arrived.

The extra power was obviously quite a draw for sportscar buyers, but by now the shape was six years old, and in the fashion car market that was very old indeed. It would not have been surprising, therefore, if the decline in sales had been halted only temporarily before a final slide into the abyss.

Yet sales rocketed to 5,443 that year, and

After 1978 the Spider ceased being an official UK import, but sales continued on continental Europe. This is a 1980 1600, featuring the new seat belt guides and revised door mirrors. By this time the 1600 also had the dash of the 2000, along with a flat luggage bay behind the seats. ALFA ROMEO ARCHIVES

although the figure dropped below 5,000 in 1973, it subsequently climbed again above this barrier. The rate of sales was now at the level it had been for the old Giulietta Spider during its best years, a fact which must have tempted Alfa into the modifications that appeared in 1980.

Not that these were extensive, in fact from the outside the 1980 Spider looked virtually identical to the 1979 model. Unless you had a door mirror fetish, you would probably be unable to tell the difference because they were the only items which had changed. Inside, however, the modifications were more noticeable. Most obvious were the seat belt guides mounted on the backrests, which were designed to prevent the webbing from slipping off occupants' shoulders. They were ugly and prominent, but necessary. Another safety-related change was made to the ignition lock, the barrel of which was re-angled to make the ignition key less wounding to knees in the event of an accident.

There was now a carpeted luggage platform behind the seats in place of the joke rear chairs – a far more realistic use of the space – and carpet for the floor instead of the drop-in rubber mats provided previously. The door trims were redesigned and featured matching armrests with tilting stowage bins beneath, though these were of limited use because they were so small it was almost impossible to get a hand into them. But at least they looked to be an improvement. The door handles and window winders were also changed for the chrome and black type used on the old 2000 GTV.

There were more substantial advances on the ergonomic front, Alfa finally coming round to moving the wiper switch to a stalk, freshly sprouting from the right-hand side of the steering column, which also triggered the washers. There was now an instrument lamp rheostat on the steering column, and leather trim had become an option, but there was little else to titivate enthusiasts. But the very fact that this 14-year-old was still alive should have been sufficient cause for pleasure.

There were no mechanical revisions, the same 102bhp 1600 and 128bhp 2000 engines being offered, driving running gear that was completely unchanged, even down to the 165–14 tyres, which were beginning to look decidedly mean for an Eighties sportscar.

The launch of these refettled Spiders, both of them known as Veloces, coincided with a general relaunch for Alfa itself, which had been going

This is a 1978 American-specification Spider at its most ugly and divergent from the European models. Painfully obvious are the colossal rubber bumpers, added in 1975 and designed to withstand 5mph impacts without damage. They did nothing for the Pininfarina lines, nor the Alfa grille, tucked on either side of the front buffer. Orange side marker lights and an ugly rear number-plate plinth were further distinguishing scars. ALFA ROMEO ARCHIVES

Mechanical differences were also considerable. The engine used Spica mechanical fuel injection from 1969 (it was replaced with a Bosch system in 1982) to provide the fuel metering accuracy necessary to meet emissions regulations, to which various extra kit including an air pump and a catalyst were gradually added, first for California, then for remaining States. The US GTV used Spica injection from 1969 until its deletion in 1974, before catalysts were demanded. The US Spiders also sat higher on softer suspension and were supplied with sump guards. ALFA ROMEO ARCHIVES

Pininfarina's Spider Aerodinamica would have been a mere footnote had the proposals within it not been taken up nine years later. Displayed at the 1974 Barcelona show, the prototype wore front and rear spoilers, wider wheels and a particularly unfortunate paint job. Drag was fractionally cut and front-end lift lowered by 47%. PININFARINA

through a particularly bad patch. Losses had been mounting, production falling, the model range ageing and quality declining. Furthermore, in northern Europe car buyers had learned the truth about Alfa bodywork; many of them had decisively slimmed wallets to prove it.

It must have come as quite a blow to the management, therefore, to see Spider sales fall catastrophically the following year. From the 5,386 cars sold in 1980, the second best figure on record, the number fell to just 1,436 – far too few to make economic sense. Alfa's response was to delete the 1600, which by this time was sold only in Europe, a move that produced just 299 sales on the home continent the following year. The remaining 2,000 or so cars went to the United States, which seemingly could always absorb a thousand or two and was the main reason for the Spider's survival.

With production at such a low level, most manufacturers would have given up at this stage. The car was old and it must have been an inconvenience for the Arese factory, whose main business was building Alfettas and Giuliettas. But instead, the car was facelifted, and it ended up looking like an experimental Spider that had been shown way back in 1974 at the Barcelona motor show.

The car was actually part of Pininfarina's rather than Alfa's display, and it was intended to stress the fact that the coachbuilder now had a full-size wind-tunnel (in fact, this had been opened two years earlier) and to demonstrate some of the results that could be achieved from it. The Spider was chosen presumably because Pininfarina had had a hand in its design and assembly, and perhaps because it might be seen as rather a hopeless case aerodynamically. Convertibles are not well-known for their atmosphere-penetrating abilities.

Apart from having a two-tone paint job, the Spider Aerodinamica flaunted a deep chin spoiler and a rubber lip on the tail which continued on to the wings. Neither of these growths did much for its looks, but the Cd figure was said to have fallen by 8.7% (Pininfarina did not reveal from what figure, which was probably a wise move) and front-end lift was reduced by 46%, rather more of an achievement.

There was nothing miraculous about this car, and today it would have been completely forgotten had its appendages not turned up nine years later on the next facelift. They helped the new Spider to a higher top speed – it was now claimed to be 118mph – although they did little for its grace and beauty. The standing-kilometre time was unaltered at 30.8sec. The car's power output remained at 128bhp at 5,300rpm, and maximum torque was also virtually unchanged at 132lb/ft.

A 1600 model remained in the range – it produced 104bhp and gave 105lb/ft at an impressively low 2,900rpm – and was good for 112mph and a standing-kilometre time of 32.8sec, a slight improvement on the 109mph and 33.3sec claimed for the old and, at 110bhp, more powerful 1600. Frankly, though, these performance changes were too small to be noticeable.

More obvious was the Spider's changed appearance, despite minimal alterations to the sheet metal. It was now topped and tailed by a pair of black plastic bumpers capped with brushed aluminium, and the beautiful grille of past editions had been supplanted by a cheap plastic triangle that was a crude and ugly insult compared to what had been there before.

The front indicator and sidelight units were mounted in the bumper, and beneath it was Pininfarina's spoiler finished in body colour. The only other changes to the front were the removal of the Perspex headlamp fairings, the addition of a plastic scoop over the air intake to improve heater throughput, and an aerial element in the front screen, a surprisingly hi-tech solution to

find in so old a car.

At the other end the bootlid was now capped by a black rubber spoiler, as were the trailing edges of the rear wings. The panel beneath was now finished in matt black to match, and a completely new set of lamp clusters which included fog-guard lamps was sunk within it. Badging was changed, too, the Spider name at last appearing on the car, together with a 2.0 or 1.6 tag.

Inside the car, the chief change was that everything that had previously been chromed was now matt black in keeping with the fashion of the time. The bezels around the three minor instruments, the detailing on the centre console, and the speedo, tacho and warning light surrounds had all gone monochromatic, as had the spokes of the wood-rimmed steering wheel.

But the architecture of the interior had barely changed at all. The facia and instruments were the same, as were the seats and door casings, and if the centre console had altered, it was not by much. It now carried a battery of warning lights just ahead of the gearlever, where they were well out of the line of sight. These were for brake fluid

The facelifted 1983 Spider featuring new bumpers, a nasty plastic dummy grille and the front and rear spoilers that were largely unchanged from the Aerodinamica prototype. PININFARINA

This detail of the tail shows the rubber three-part rear spoiler, the new tail-lamps and the bigger rear bumper. Matt black did not suit the car. IAN DAWSON

level (new to the Spider because the law demanded it), handbrake on, choke out, oil pressure, main beam and sidelights, and they looked like untidy afterthoughts.

Beneath the gearlever, now capped by a wood-effect knob, was a digital clock and the fan switch, and below these a bank of four switches or, to be more accurate, two switches and two blanking plates, because only the hazard warning lights and rear foglamps were triggered from here. Behind them, at the end of the console, was just a choke knob, the hand throttle having been deleted. Other detail trivia included a redesigned ashtray, the appearance of the latest Alfa badge in the steering wheel boss and a courtesy light delay.

Mechanical changes were even more minimal, consisting of a change for the 2-litre to 185/70-section tyres (at last, something slightly more modern, though hardly leading-edge sportscar rubberware) and a reduction in fuel tank capacity from 51 to 46 litres.

Little money had been spent on the facelift, but it was quite effective in terms of signalling a change – the Spider unquestionably looked more modern. It was just unfortunate that it ended up resembling an ageing fashion victim. The Spider was too old to wear matt black, moulded bumpers and body-colour spoilers, but it was clearly too young to die. After another shaky year in 1982, when only 2,274 Spiders were produced, output swelled to 5,430 and set a new record. The bulk of these were sold in Europe, though the following year the US market took the majority, some 3,341 cars out of a total of 6,177, itself another production record. So the facelift had paid off.

There was good news in Britain, too. Though Alfa Romeo still considered the Spider to be not worth importing – the UK company was pushing Alfa saloons heavily around this time – Surrey-based dealers Bell and Colvill disagreed. They had become Alfa dealers in 1970, but had given up the franchise in 1983 because they no longer considered it viable. However, they had detected a small and continuing demand for Spiders and so had begun unofficially to import them in 1979, only a year after Alfa GB had stopped bringing them in.

The numbers were very low initially, and only a couple of these were converted to right-hand drive. But in 1984 demand began to take off, stimulated by press reports of the converted car and by regular advertising. It was not long before the dealership was selling between 50 and 100 Spiders a year, the vast majority of which were converted to right-hand drive. These cars came from Alfa dealers in Holland, France and Germany and were brought in on a personal import basis, thus avoiding the problems of Type Approval, though the cars nevertheless conformed to the broad European Community regulations.

It was one of these machines that *CAR Magazine* tested in 1985 in a comparison with the new but rather mis-shapen Reliant Scimitar SS1. This is what Gavin Green had to say of the Alfa: 'Lower yourself onto the rather stark vinyl seats and you'll notice the decidedly simian driving position – which will have old Alfa aficionados weeping with nostalgia, but more pragmatic folk weeping with frustration. The ultimate in the long arm/short leg Italian school of seating positions is exacerbated by the large diameter wheel which hinders the amount of room for acutely bent knees.

'Your horror at the seating position will soon be swept away, though, when you summon the engine into life. Give the accelerator pedal a

The interior was much the same as before except that there was plenty of matt black. At least the wheel was still wood-rimmed. This is a 1985 Bell and Colvill right-hand-drive conversion. IAN DAWSON

couple of jabs, turn the key, then settle back for one of the finest mechanical musicals ever to reverberate in the cockpit of a car.

'The 127bhp, 131lb/ft long-stroke design gets raucous at high revs – the red hue of the tacho begins at 5,700rpm, although at much over 5,000 there are signs of mechanical strain – yet the amazing flexibility of the motor in the lower-to-mid-rev ranges more than compensates for this high-revving bout of asthma.

'The handling impresses, too. Despite pronounced scuttle shake over road irregularities and despite rather archaic recirculating-ball steering, the lack of precision of which is exacerbated by the big steering wheel, the Alfa is a sharp and taut performer on winding roads. It is eminently predictable, turns into bends obediently and holds the road well – helped by larger tyres than was the case with pre-'78 Spiders. They're now 185/70HR-14s. The ride is acceptable, although the rear axle can get lively – and the suspension is undeniably firm. Other driver appeal bonuses are the superbly placed pedals – ideal for heel and toe gearchanges – and the manoeuvrable feel the car imparts.

'. . . the fact that the Spider is still in demand today is evidence of its enduring appeal, and of its character. Some aspects of the car are decidedly senescent – like that driving position. But in most ways, the Alfa has aged surprisingly well. It is still the most desirable £11,000-or-less open-top sportscar. The fact that, for my money, it is also the most desirable current Alfa says a lot about the character of '60s examples of the marque –

and a lot about the company's slide since.'

By this time Alfa had slid a long way, too, into loss, dwindling sales and plenty of other troubles. Spider sales held up, though, and so the car was treated to another facelift, this one coming at the 1986 Geneva show, exactly 20 years after the car's launch. There were redesigned interiors for the 2.0 and 1.6, but most attention was focussed on a new version based on the 2.0 and called the Quadrifoglio Verde, after the four-leaf clover that had appeared on all of Alfa's racers since the early days.

The reason for the attention was to be found hanging from the lower reaches of the car's flanks, where some of the most grotesque sill extensions yet fitted to a car were on view. They might have been trendy, but they suited the Spider's rounded lines about as well as a mohican haircut would have suited a monk.

There were also alterations to the nose and tail, the front end getting a new spoiler that blended rather more successfully than the old, and the rear end a matching fairing beneath the bumper. The QV was fitted with fatter 195/60HR-15 tyres to suit its more aggressive mien and the alloy wheels were of a new design. There was also a new hardtop, one that looked considerably more modern than the original, largely because of the perforated black insert that hooped over the top, although visibility suffered for this stylistic flourish. The hardtop was lined and it came with an interior light and, better still, a heated rear window.

Lesser exterior changes, which also applied to the other models in the range, included new door mirrors, a different Pininfarina badge on the rear flanks and the removal of the tiny chrome ear from the fuel filler flap because this now opened remotely. The 2.0 remained on the 14in five-spoke alloy wheels first seen at the previous facelift and the 1.6 was still mounted on steel wheels.

There were big changes inside for all three cars, the dashboard being cleverly reworked to look very different and decidedly more modern, despite the fact that the basic facia moulding was retained. The speedometer and tachometer were replaced by a single sizeable housing that contained both instruments as well as the oil pressure, battery condition and temperature gauges and various warning lights.

In the recess where previously there had been three minor dials there were now three air vents, while additional padding, necessitated by American internal protection regulations, was provided along the bottom edge of the facia. The steering wheel was new and rather ugly, the wood rim having been replaced by a leather-clad item and the boss enlarged to the size of a small sponge cake, which looked as silly as it sounds.

The centre console was tidied up considerably now that all the warning lights were housed in the instrument pack, and apart from the gearlever, which was now capped by a leather-bound knob, it simply contained the heater slides, the fan switch (returned to its original location in the top left corner) and a redesigned digital clock. Behind lay an altered tunnel console containing the ashtray and a set of new push/push buttons for the rear foglamps, the electric windows and the

hazard lights.

Door trims and much of the other detail remained unchanged, but there were new seats with longer cushions and deeper lateral bolstering for more support. The QV's leather seats were stitched in a contrasting colour, which did quite a lot to reinforce the impression that this was a high-class car. Though some might have regretted the loss of the old interior's style, there was no doubt that Pininfarina had managed a dramatically effective update without changing too many parts. Visually, at least, the Spider was hiding its years well.

Unfortunately, the same could not be true of the driving experience, which was bound to be undermined by the car's dated mechanicals, to which only minimal modifications had been made. Indeed, they amounted to no more than the introduction of electronic ignition on the 2.0. However, there was now a catalyst-equipped version on sale in certain European markets, which used Bosch L-Jetronic fuel injection, though this sophistication was insufficient to restore performance to the level achieved by the carburettor model, power having dropped from 128bhp to 115bhp.

Nevertheless, these changes gave sales another boost, even though in 1985, the year before they were introduced, Alfa had produced 5,286 cars, making it one of the Spider's better seasons. But the figure rose to 7,015 following the facelift, which meant that the Spider's 20th year was its best ever. Over 4,000 cars went to the US, which

The engine of the same 1985 car looked much as it had been when the 2000 first appeared. Power had dropped, but only slightly, to 127bhp. The large crossbar at the rear of the engine was part of the linkage for the right-hand-drive conversion. Despite the apparent crudity of this solution, the steering feel was surprisingly precise and taut. IAN DAWSON

There was another facelift for the car in 1986, this one bringing an updated interior and the Quadrifoglio Verde model to supplement the 1.6 and 2.0 models. The QV came with skirts all round, new alloy wheels on 195/60-15 tyres and featured a new hardtop. The lesser models did without the skirts, but picked up such interior alterations and refinements as the remote-control fuel flap release. ALFA ROMEO ARCHIVES

was also a record, though the European figure of 2,626 scarcely made it a vintage season in this market. There could be no doubt, though, that the Spider was well worth keeping in production.

In 1988, however, complete manufacture of the car was transferred to Pininfarina's assembly operations in Turin, the coachbuilders having previously been responsible only for the body-work and interior. Visiting the plant after the changeover, one was confronted by the unusual sight of Spiders, Peugeot 205 cabriolets, Lancia Thema estates, tractor cabs and Ferrari Testarossa bodies all coming through the same paint shops and down the same assembly line.

By 1989, production had begun to dwindle somewhat, and was once again below 4,000 units. Clearly, it was time for another facelift. The tactic had been successful before, despite the fact that other manufacturers around the world had been claiming there was no longer a market for soft-top sportscars. Now there were some new open cars in the market, such as the Mazda MX-5, which could only stimulate interest in the breed. Though the little Mazda was a vastly more modern car than the Spider, and vastly more

competent as a result, it was a high-volume machine that was unlikely to threaten the relative trickle of Spiders coming from Pininfarina.

So, in January 1990, the latest facelift was launched at the Detroit and Los Angeles auto shows and it made its European debut two months later at the Geneva show, some 24 years after the Alfa two-seater was first shown there. Few, if any, cars have been treated to facelifts at this age, but the Spider is up there with the Beetle, the Mini and the 2CV as one of the great survivors, even if its sales figures cannot challenge the records of this trio.

The changes were at least as extensive as they had been in 1970 when the Spider's tail was lopped off. When the car finally dies, this facelift may well be considered to have been as successful. This time the scalpel was wielded with a sensitivity that escaped the designers who performed the 1983 facelift, and the result is vastly more pleasing, successfully combining the car's familiar profile with modern detail solutions.

Once again the main changes were made at the rear, and they involved new pressings for the bootlid, rear wings and rear panel, the object being

From the front, at least, the QV looked neater, the new spoiler being more tidily integrated with the bumper. The cheap plastic grille remained, though. Just visible is the scoop over the heater air intake ahead of the wipers. ALFA ROMEO ARCHIVES

to echo a design theme of the 164 saloon and the then-new 33, in which the thin strip of rear lamps traversed the full width of the car. The bootlid was kicked up slightly at its trailing edge to create a modest spoiler (no word on whether it was actually effective) and a large badge lay just ahead of it.

Completely new bumpers were fitted, this time moulded in impact-absorbing plastic, shrouding the entire lower sections of the car and painted in body colour, tidying up its appearance considerably. The front bumper incorporated the Alfa shield and a lower air intake, again sculpted to mirror the shapes found on the noses of the 164 and 33, while the indicator/sidelight assemblies were also bumper-mounted. And still there was nowhere to mount a front numberplate.

There were no changes at the front end above bumper level, the Spider continuing to do without Perspex headlamp covers. However, there were reshaped, body-colour door mirrors and new oval side repeater flashers on the rear halves of the front wings. The sills continued to be skirt-clad, but this time the mouldings were vastly more subtle, blending more successfully with the bumpers and the car's flanks. Other changes included the reappearance of a conventional electric aerial on a rear wing and revised Spider 2.0 graphics on the rear panel (a 1.6 was also available in some markets). But the basic form of the car remained unchanged, as did its hardtop, which blended with this latest style rather more successfully than it had with the previous one.

There were detail changes inside, such as new carpets and the standardization of a pair of speakers, but the seats and dashboard remained essentially unaltered, along with that cumbersome, big-bossed steering wheel. Apart from the introduction of a new light tan trim colour, which did much to lift the ambiance of the cabin, the biggest changes were to the door casings, which were restyled along with their armrests. The old GTV interior door handles remained, but they were now matt black and had rubber inserts, which modernized them rather well. The seats were the same shape, but trimmed in an attractive mix of Texalfa and Alcantara, a suede-like material. Leather remained an option for the seats and steering wheel rim.

Overall, the effect was quite attractive, Pininfarina once again succeeding in updating the Spider's cabin with a minimum of change and expense. This time, however, Alfa designed to spend some money on the Spider's entrails, upgrading both the twin-cam engine and its running gear.

The 2-litre now came in two states of tune, both versions using Bosch Motronic ML 4.1 integrated ignition and fuel injection as well as Alfa's variable inlet valve timing device, which first appeared on the Alfetta saloon in the early Eighties. Hydraulics and electronic control enabled the position of the inlet cam to be changed relative to the exhaust cam, altering valve overlap and so allowing the torque curve to be further optimized. It is a clever system, though not as sophisticated (or as complex) as Honda's V-TEC set-up as used on some Civic models.

In this guise the old twin-cam delivered 126bhp at 5,800rpm, slightly less power than before, but with improved emissions performance. Peak torque was 124lb/ft at 4,200rpm, again slightly less than the 131lb/ft of the old car. The other version of the engine came with a three-way catalyst and met the USA 1983 emissions regulations, and this engine was fitted to Spiders exported to Britain. In this case power output fell to 120bhp at the same crank speed, and torque dropped to 116lb/ft, again at 4,200rpm. Alfa claimed a maximum of 118mph for both cars, the catalyst model needing 9.4sec to reach 62mph, the non-cat car 9.0sec.

These are not bad figures, but many wondered why Alfa hadn't taken the opportunity to fit the twin-spark cylinder-head used on the 75. The company claimed that it was because a convertible doesn't need to go that hard (which is true to some extent), but the real reason was probably that the chassis and brakes were not really up to

Though the dash looked radically different, the main facia moulding was unchanged apart from the extra padding at its base needed to meet American crash regulations. The new instrument binnacle was less elegant than the twin pods previously fitted, but the instruments were grouped together and very clear. A trio of air vents filled the positions vacated by the relocated minor gauges. ALFA ROMEO ARCHIVES

The Spider was facelifted again in 1990, some 24 years after its launch, and extensively. Visible here are the new front bumper and its integral grille, new side skirts, alloy wheels carried over from the QV for the 2.0 (the 1.6 had the five-spoke wheels that arrived with the 1983 facelift), and the body-coloured door mirrors and heater intake. Note that still there is nowhere properly to mount a number-plate. ALFA ROMEO ARCHIVES

the twin-spark's 148bhp, as the test of a 1991 Spider suggests towards the back of this book.

The 1.6-litre engine, which was available only in Italy, Greece and Portugal, was much the same as it had always been bar the addition of electronic ignition. It did without the variable valve timing system and it retained twin-choke Weber carburettors to deliver 109bhp, an increase of 6bhp and enough to restore it to its earlier peak. Top speed was 112mph and the 0–62mph sprint was completed in 10sec.

With its lower power output the 1.6 version did without a front anti-roll bar and wore smaller tyres than the 2-litre models (it also had a vinyl rather than a cotton hood), but it did get the new ZF power steering system introduced with this facelift. The steering gear, incidentally, could still be either recirculating-ball or worm-and-roller, depending on the supplier. Apart from this, the running gear of all three models remained fundamentally the same, though there were some very minor geometry modifications and alterations to the brakes, and the 2-litre cars were fitted with a limited-slip differential as standard as well as fatter 195/60HR-15 tyres.

So that was the Spider of the Nineties, with

The rear end was completely new, the style being designed to mimic the themes of the Alfa Romeo 164 and 33 rear ends, complete with full-width rear lamps. The rear wings and bootlid were new pressings, and there was a new bumper. This treatment was far more attractive than the previous restyle. ALFA ROMEO ARCHIVES

The 1.6, which was sold in certain European markets, with its starfish alloy wheels. The facelift did much to tidy the Spider's appearance. The 1.6 used a 109bhp carburettor version of the 1570 twin-cam, and like the 2-litre it came with ZF power steering. The 2-litre models had either an injected 126bhp engine or, in the case of the UK and US markets, an injected catalyst unit of 120bhp. ALFA ROMEO ARCHIVES

four facelifts and a long career behind it. It is still stylish, still desirable, still fun to drive, and, as I write, still in production. According to those in the know, it still has a few years left – the curtain is not scheduled to drop before 1995, when a new Spider is at last due to arrive. That car, one understands, will be based on the 75, a distant successor to the 1962 Giulia saloon. The new Spider will be front-wheel driven, built at Arese and fitted with the 2-litre twin-spark motor, a direct descendant of the Spider's own 2-litre engine, as well as Alfa's wonderful V6. It will doubtless prove a success, but it is unlikely to lead the charmed life of the car it succeeds, which, when finally it is laid to rest, will have lived for almost three decades.

CHAPTER 10

Derivations and variations

One might think, given the already exotic character of the Giulia GT and the Spider, that Alfa would have no need to introduce yet more specialized derivatives of its saloon cars. Yet during the life of both the Giulietta and the Giulia saloons, limited runs of some outstandingly beautiful postwar sportscars emerged from coachbuilders' workshops in Turin.

Among these were the Giulietta SZ racer, the ultra-aerodynamic SS, the racing TZs and, in the early Seventies, the Junior Zs. Then there were the GTAs, competition versions of the Giulia Sprint GTs which would eventually spawn some astonishingly powerful race cars, and the amazing Montreal which, although it used a V8 engine, was based on a 105-series coupe chassis that, unfortunately for the car's career, just wasn't up to the job.

Though it started life built on a Giulietta platform, the SS later appeared based on Giulia running gear, which is why it appears here. The SZ was related to the Giulias only in being an influential ancestor, but it is included because it was a sister car to the SS. In spite of their extreme specification, the TZs were very much part of the Giulia family, as well as being precursors of the GTAs.

It is beyond the scope of this book to deal with each of these cars exhaustively, so what follows is an outline of the background and composition of each model. Be warned, though, that if you have the misfortune to be stricken by the Alfa virus and are restricted by a slender wallet, learning about these cars is going to be agony.

The Giulietta SS as originally proposed by Bertone's design chief Scaglione. Its grille was Ferrari-like, doing without the Alfa shield, and the tail ended in a taper, whereas the production version's rear end was abruptly truncated to contain its length. Early cars did without front bumpers and used Plexiglass side windows, but had an Alfa grille. The prototype car was aluminium-bodied over an aluminium spaceframe with a plastic floor. Production cars were steel-bodied. ALFA ROMEO ARCHIVES

A production Giulietta 1300 SS with front bumper and the curious deflector just ahead of the windscreen, intended to prevent wiper lift at speed. A striking design, some consider the SS flawed because the roofline rises too high, which was necessitated by the lack of headroom in the prototype. The car was as aerodynamic as it looks, with a Cd of around 0.28, the same as the aerodynamically lauded Vauxhall Calibra of the Nineties. ALFA ROMEO ARCHIVES

ALFA ROMEO GIULIETTA SPRINT SPECIALE

The SS looks like the car Buck Rogers would drive. Its long, fluent lines and improbably curvaceous screen gave it the look of a show car and the legs of a machine with a far larger heart. It was built by Bertone according to aerodynamic principles which the coachbuilder had been investigating for Alfa during the 1900-based BAT project, and the result was a 1,300cc car that could muster 124mph, an achievement that at the time of writing no current 1300 approaches.

The car was designed by Bertone's chief designer, Franco Scaglione, and it first appeared in prototype form at the 1957 Turin show, clothed in aluminium and, with its plastic windows and minimal interior trim, obviously intended for competition work. It was quoted as having a 100bhp 1300 motor and a new five-speed gearbox, but other details were scant.

Production versions appeared a year later, and they were much changed, having steel rather than aluminium bodywork, shortened front and rear overhangs and a taller roof, the overall height of the original car being so low that it was almost impossible to climb inside wearing a crash helmet. Not that Bertone seemed to be pushing the SS's race potential any more because with its steel shell it now weighed much the same as a Giulietta Sprint.

The reason for the change of tack was almost certainly the arrival of the alloy-bodied Zagato SZ, which seemed to promise racing drivers more than the SS, and the Bertone car's fully trimmed interior served to confirm the fact.

Its chief advantages over the Sprint – apart from its looks – were a reduced frontal area, a low-drag body, a floor-mounted five-speed gearshift and a slightly more powerful 100bhp 1,290cc Veloce engine, the extra 10bhp being gained by altering the valve timing and reducing the valve clearances. But high prices limited demand; in Britain, for example, the car cost as much as an Aston Martin DB3 or a Porsche Carrera, which meant that you had to want one very badly in order to justify buying it.

The Beatles' John Lennon is reputed to have been an owner, which perhaps is an indication of the kind of spare money required to buy a car like this. It could be an apocryphal story, but Lennon is said to have loved the car so much that when the time came for a change he had it crushed into a bale small enough to put in his home as a permanent reminder. If true it was a waste of a beautiful car, without doubt, but at least it had been appreciated.

The SS was not all about looks, however. Though no Cd figure has ever been quoted, it has been extrapolated as being in the region of 0.27 to 0.28, which is about what the best production cars of the early Nineties manage. Nuccio Bertone claimed to be 'profoundly satisfied with the car from every standpoint. Its aerodynamic qualities are truly excellent. The structural integration of the design is such that not a body being made today has greater torsional rigidity.'

An *Autosport* road test of a very early SS quoted its top speed as 124.8mph, though this was with one of the first 100 cars, which were lighter and shaped more aerodynamically than later cars. Known as the low-nose models, they did without front bumpers and had plexiglass side windows. The SS was modified again in 1960 when Alfa decided to expand production from Bertone's plant, where the cars were built.

The SS gained a front bumper, a longer boot opening, raised headlights (necessitated by American regulations) and a higher nose. The roof was raised by 1½in and weight went up by 143lb, not that this changed the basic character of the car, which excelled as a long-distance tourer, despite its diminutive engine. The low-drag shell and five-speed gearbox allowed unstressed high-speed cruising over long distances, too, because the 17.5-gallon fuel tank gave the car a range of over 500 miles. Moreover, a journey of this length was a realistic proposition because the SS was

uncannily quiet. It was not merely that wind roar was so extraordinarily muted, as might have been hoped for with so sylph-like a shape, but that road and exhaust noises were also better contained than in the Giulietta. Another advantage offered by the SS was exceptional visibility thanks to the car's deep screens and slender pillars.

In other respects the car was much the same as a Giulietta Sprint, which meant agile and entertaining handling, above-average brakes and a responsive, rev-to-the-heavens engine. Some 1,366 cars were built before the 1300 was replaced in March 1963 by a second series, this time using the Giulia 1600 engine, which gave the car a power output of 112bhp.

Other modifications included a change to disc brakes at the front, altered gear ratios, a revised dashboard and new badging. In this form the SS lived for another two years, during which time Bertone built a further 1,400 examples, which still makes the SS a rare car. Despite this, and its ground-breaking aerodynamics and stunning shape, this model has not been as revered as some considerably more prosaic machinery and it was only at the start of the Nineties that prices began to move sharply upwards. Yet the SS remains one of the greatest Alfas from the Sixties.

In 1963 the Giulietta SS became the Giulia SS, primary gains being the 1600 engine, disc front brakes and a revised dashboard. External clues were minimal, though, being limited to badging and detail like the revised side repeaters.

The 1961 Zagato SZ was an aluminium-bodied, spaceframe Giulietta that weighed 200lb less than the Sprint. Built on the Spider's shorter wheelbase, the SZ was conceived for competition work, leading to the creation of 30 very quick Kamm-tailed derivatives at the end of the 210-strong production run. It was in one of these cars that Elio Zagato and designer Ercole Spada recorded a 141mph top speed on the Milan–Bergamo autostrada, an amazing speed for a 1,300cc car. ALFA ROMEO ARCHIVES

ALFA ROMEO GIULIETTA SZ

Zagato built only 210 SZs. Nevertheless, this is the ultimate sporting Giulietta, being easily the quickest because it weighed so little – 1,890lb compared to the 2,220lb of the SS and the 2,090lb of the Sprint, according to *Road & Track*. Top speed was not far behind that of the SS, and its 0–60mph time was 11.2sec as opposed to 12.3sec. The standard 92bhp Sprint managed to reach 103mph and 0–60mph in 13.2sec, figures which underline its aerodynamic inferiority.

It is easy to see, therefore, that the SZ was Alfa's best bet for racing, and indeed it was the company's desire to return to the track that led to what was a relatively large production run for so specialized a car.

The SZ started life as a Zagato-built special, the inspiration for which came from Elio Zagato himself, who happened to be an enthusiastic racer and wanted a car in which he could compete more effectively. Realizing the potential of the SZ, and that the heavier steel-bodied SS was not sufficiently competitive to bring results, Alfa commissioned Zagato to build a run of SZs that culminated in a final batch of 30 long-nose, Kamm-tail models with an astonishingly high top speed.

The SZ was light largely because of its body construction. It was built on the Giulietta Spider's 88.5in wheelbase floor, but it used a close-mesh, small-bore tubular framework to support the ultra-light aluminium panelling. Minimal interior trim, a glassfibre dashboard, plexiglass side windows, lightweight seats,

The SZ's shape looks aerodynamically clean, as indeed it proved to be. Note the Plexiglas headlamp covers, Zagato being one of the earliest users of the material. SZs were handbuilt and expensive, needing over 300 hours to complete. ALFA ROMEO ARCHIVES

The Giulia TZ, undoubtedly the most desirable postwar production Alfa. Prices are sky-high, not least because only 112 were made. Built on a tubular spaceframe by Zagato (hence TZ), it used the 112bhp 1,570cc twin-cam engine, though race versions developed as much as 170bhp at 7,600rpm. ALFA ROMEO ARCHIVES

aluminium headlamp rims and screen surrounds and extraordinarily light doors contributed to the weight-paring. Mechanically it was basically the same as for the Giulietta apart from its more potent, 112bhp engine – the same as in the SS – and the use of Campagnolo alloy wheels.

The SZ was the most agile of the Giuliettas and the most stiffly sprung. It cornered with minimal roll, delicate steering inputs and amazing finesse, though its short wheelbase and minimal overhangs could make it a twitchy handful in the wet. Like the SS it had an enormous fuel tank, but long journeys were more wearing, the seats being not a lot softer than the average park bench, while it was fairly clear that high-speed refinement had not been a priority during the car's conception. But then, the SZ was a racer.

It was a bid to improve its competitiveness that led Alfa to put an SZ into the wind-tunnel in an effort to reduce drag. Experimentation produced the longer nose and stretched Kamm tail, changes which considerably altered the car's original very rounded profile, as well as its top speed, which climbed from 124mph to over 150mph. A further 30lb was pared away, the engine was coaxed into delivering an additional 10bhp, and disc brakes were fitted at the front.

Inevitably, these cars are immensely rare today and are avidly hunted by collectors. Consequently,

their price tags are likely to be such as to dissuade all but the super-rich.

ALFA ROMEO GIULIA GTZ

The GTZ is unmistakably the son of the last SZs. Conceived entirely for racing, the TZ, as it became better known, went on sale in 1963, although work on it had begun as early as 1959 and the first prototype was manufactured in 1960. The launch was delayed while the company gave priority to the commercially crucial Giulias as well as the 2600 series.

Alfa repeatedly found that using its production car engineers to develop race cars was a problem because frequently they would have to abandon their race projects in order to deal with more urgent mainstream concerns. This was not the way to proceed in the ultra-competitive racing world, so as the TZ programme dragged on in fits and starts, Alfa decided to establish separate racing operations which could be devoted full-time to such exploits.

Assembly of the 100 TZs needed for homologation was entrusted to an Alfa dealer in Udine, near Venice, and the Chizzola brothers who ran it dubbed the operation Delta. At the same time, Alfa set up a race preparation unit in Milan to fettle the cars and enter them in races.

Though it looked like a direct descendent of the SZ, the TZ began concurrently as a separate project of Alfa's, rather than Zagato's. But Zagato was given the job of building the prototypes because of the company's experience with tubular construction, and subsequently built the production car bodies. The indented trefoil-shaped rear was formed for maximum aerodynamic efficiency, helping the standard cars to an amazing 134mph top speed. This car is a 1963 model, chassis number 002. ALFA ROMEO ARCHIVES

Eventually it was decided that the two operations should be amalgamated and located in Milan, where Autodelta, as it was now called, would be close to the factory. In 1966, this outfit became an integral part of Alfa, with Carlo Chiti as its director general, the well-known ex-Ferrari Formula One engineer having joined the company in 1963 in order to help develop the GTZ.

The initials stood for Giulia Tubolare Zagato, and the car's spaceframe construction was designed by Alfa's Edo Mazoni, who provided a complex weave of tubes to form a skeleton that weighed just 88lb. It was immensely strong, and it carried mountings for the double-wishbone front suspension and a rear suspension that incorporated lower wishbones, transverse upper radius arms and coil springs. The GTZ became the first postwar Alfa to have independent rear suspension. The standard engine was the 112bhp 1,570cc twin-cam unit used in the SS and SZ, though race-tuned versions of it would eventually be good for 170bhp at a shrieking 7,600rpm. The engine was canted over at a considerable angle, necessitating the use of a special bellhousing to allow it to mate with the

five-speed gearbox. Girling disc brakes were fitted all round, the rear rotors being mounted inboard to reduce unsprung weight.

The Zagato bodywork was very much a development of the Kamm-tailed SZ style. Again, the car was extremely light, weighing just 1,452lb, and it was capable of 134mph with its standard road-going engine, proving once again that, during this era at least, Alfa Romeo was a master of aerodynamics. Wind-tunnel tests led to the Kamm tail being developed still further, it becoming recessed, and because of the car's unusual rear cross-section it formed a trefoil, giving the GTV a very distinctive appearance.

Just 112 GTZs were built, to be followed by a final run of 12 glassfibre-bodied versions, all of which were used by Alfa's Autodelta racing offshoot. The last dozen, which were built in 1965, had a lower spaceframe that necessitated a redesign of the body, the object being to reduce the frontal area. The engines of these cars used a twin-plug cylinder-head and produced 175bhp at 7,600rpm.

Despite considerable success on the circuits, development of the GTZ stopped at this point because rule changes allowed Alfa to contest a machine that was much closer, in appearance if not in spirit, to one of its volume production models. That car was the GTA.

ALFA ROMEO GIULIA GTA

The GTA made its debut at the 1965 Amsterdam show, but it would have been far more appropriate if it had been launched at a racing car show. This model would turn out to be one of the most formidable saloon racers of the Sixties, earning sufficient laurels to hedge a decent garden.

The A stood for alleggerita – lightened – and though the car looked much like any other Sprint GT it was in fact very different. The biggest change was the most subtle of all – all the external bodywork was fabricated from aluminium rather than steel, and pop-riveted to the under-structure. Sound-deadening was given the heave-

ho, as were the armrests, the side windows were plexiglass and many of the cabin fittings went on a diet, the end result being 603lb shed from the 2,244lb 1600 GTV, an amazing feat of paring.

The 1,570cc engine was heavily modified, the standard cylinder-head being ditched in favour of a twin-plug design, the removal of the single plug from the centre of the combustion chamber allowing the use of larger valves. The additional plug was needed to restore the mixture ignition characteristics to the efficiency of the single-plug arrangement. The eight plugs were fired by a single distributor, which had a very complex looking cap as a consequence.

The larger valves and a compression ratio of 9.7:1 generated 115bhp at 6,000rpm, which was sufficient for a top speed of 115mph. But that was only the start. Autodelta could also supply a corsa engine – the word means racing – that delivered up to 170bhp and gave the car a top speed of over

The GTA superseded the TZ as Alfa's main race weapon in 1965. Outwardly similar to the standard Sprint, it had aluminium bodywork, stamped on the same presses used for the steel panels, to save weight, a twin-plug cylinder head and, for racing, the addition of a sliding block to the rear suspension, an axle-mounted tongue sliding vertically in a grooved block firmly fixed to the body to provide additional location. Andrea de Adamich is seen driving this car at the Nurburgring in 1967 on the way to fourth place and a class win. ALFA ROMEO ARCHIVES

The interior of the GTA looked much the same as the standard Sprint GT's, the chief difference being the drilled, three-spoke, wood-rim wheel. Exterior identification was limited to lightweight door handles, the unique lattice grille, a triangular four-leafed clover sticker on the front wings and no hubcaps. ALFA ROMEO ARCHIVES

This more aggressive-looking GTA is actually the less potent 1300 Junior version, announced in 1968, of which 447 were built. Its short-stroke, high-revving twin-plug 1300 engine produced 96bhp, though Autodelta-tuned versions were good for 160bhp. ALFA ROMEO ARCHIVES

135mph. A 10.5:1 compression ratio, smaller valves, polished ports and a rev limit of 7,500rpm were the key features.

The standard GTA came with shorter gearing, 14in rather than 15in wheels and modified suspension, but again this could be added to if racing was the aim. Options included a limited-slip differential, an oil cooler, a big-bore exhaust, 7in wide alloy wheels, a rear anti-roll bar, additional lateral location for the back axle as well as a raised roll-centre, a 20-gallon fuel tank, competition seats, a heavy-duty clutch and a roll-cage. Another 100lb would be shorn from the car

before this extra kit was added. All of this would have cost the owner a lot of money (two-thirds as much as the basic car, in fact) but it would have provided a car capable of winning its class in the 1966 Touring Car Championship, as indeed the GTA duly did. You can read more about this in Chapter 11.

The first run of 500 GTAs was built over a three-year period from 1966, 50 of the cars having right-hand drive. During the same period Autodelta also built 10 highly specialized GTAs for the Group 5 Championship, the objective being outright wins. This version was known as the GTA-SA (for sovralimentato) and it used superchargers to boost power to a startling 220bhp at 7,500rpm, and all from 1,570cc. The method of summoning the extra horsepower was somewhat complex, however.

Two centrifugal superchargers were used in combination with two twin-choke carburettors, and they were driven indirectly, via a chain-driven hydraulic pump that drove two turbines, these in turn motivating the blowers, which could spin to 10,000rpm.

This complicated approach seems to have been taken with the aim of separating blower speed from crank speed. Centrifugal blowers generate little boost at low rpm, but deliver instead a huge belt of assistance as the revs climb high, which could be a little too thrilling for a driver who encountered it while already cornering on the limit. The arrangement described was an attempt to get around this problem.

But it was not the only unusual feature of the engine, which also featured water injection of the inlet manifold to produce a more dense and therefore more potent fuel/air charge, as well as some interesting rearrangement of its internal architecture. Although it was still, in approximate terms, a 1,570cc engine, this twin-cam's displacement was actually 1,568cc rather than the 1,567cc which was the accurate figure for the standard unit, the modest difference coming from the larger bore and shorter stroke chosen to reduce piston speed. Larger inlet valves were also installed. The GTA-SA weighed a fraction more than the standard GTA at 1,716lb, but this did not impede its near-150mph top speed.

Not that this GTA was the most potent of the breed, but before an even more powerful beast arrived, Autodelta produced a GTA with a 1300 engine designed to contest the smaller capacity classes. It was announced in June 1968 and was instantly identifiable by its white side stripes, a pair of large four-leaf clovers on the front wings and an even larger serpent on the bonnet.

Like the original 1600 version, it was lightened and given a twin-plug cylinder-head, but this time the bore and stroke dimensions were altered from 74 x 75mm to 78 x 67.5mm, the shorter stroke producing a much higher-revving motor of 1,290cc. Power climbed to 96bhp at 6,000rpm from the 89bhp of the standard car, and top speed was 109mph, but the Autodelta versions would reach 130mph with the help of an engine tuned to deliver 160bhp at 7,800rpm. Then a batch of 100 were built with Spica mechanical fuel injection

rather than twin carburettors, and they were able to deliver 165bhp at a sensational 8,400rpm.

In total, 447 GTA 1300s were made between 1968 and 1972, some 300 of them being competition versions prepared by Autodelta. But the GTA's development was far from over yet. Bigger engines were on the way, though strictly speaking they were not housed in GTAs because

The GTA looked wonderfully purposeful when bumperless, a condition exposing the subtle sweep of the front wings into the valance. Further identifying features included the extra air intakes below the grille and, just visible on the bonnet, an enormous white serpent. From the rear the wraparound of the side stripes and the large lettering on the bootlid marked the car. Note that this one wears bumpers. ALFA ROMEO ARCHIVES

A GT-Am bears down on a GTA 1300 at Brno, in Czechoslovakia. This shot shows the sizeable extra width of the GT-Ams, which were considerably more powerful, running 1,985cc engines. ALFA ROMEO ARCHIVES

a modified version of the standard steel shell was used rather than the lightweight aluminium-clad version. But a towering reputation had grown around the GTA designation, and so it lived on, first in the 1750 GTAm.

The Am part of the name stemmed from the fact that the car was based on the American-specification version of the 1750 GTV, which used Spica fuel injection for emissions reasons, and therefore enabled the racer also to use the injection system. The 1,779cc motor was bored out to produce 1,985cc, the twin-plug head was installed and 220bhp (SAE as no DIN figure is available) emerged from the flywheel at 7,200rpm, a sizeable increase on the standard 1750's 118bhp (DIN) and sufficient for the car to reach 136mph. That was in 1970. The following year the same car was renamed the 2000 GTAm because the production version was now known as a 2-litre, though its capacity did not change. The power

output did, however, climbing to as much as 240bhp SAE and allowing the car to reach a maximum speed of 143mph. Just 40 GTAms were built, all of them for race use.

They were a dramatic sight, even when stationary, their massive tyres shrouded by glassfibre wing extensions that were simply pop-riveted to the cut-back steel wings, which gave the cars a messy look, even when they were factory-fresh. There were no bumpers, and the exhaust poked out from just beneath the driver's door. But if they looked a little unprofessional, their race results were anything but, the GTAms collecting for Alfa a substantial number of outright wins as distinct from the class victories normally associated with the GTAs.

So, with production stopping just short of the 1,000 mark at 996 units, the GTAs and GTAms concluded a run during which derivatives of the Sprint GT had been at or near the top of saloon

A GT-Am, driven by Toine Hezemans, at the Monza Four Hours in 1970, which the car won. This car looks tidier than many of the 40 GT-Ams, which had their wheelarch extensions pop-riveted on to house the larger wheels and tyres. By 1972 the engine was producing 240bhp, though that was good for no more than 140mph, proving the relative aerodynamic inefficiency of the design compared with the SZ and TZ. ALFA ROMEO ARCHIVES

car racing for six years, which was a formidable achievement.

ALFA ROMEO JUNIOR Z

The Junior Z was a Zagato-built successor to the SZ and TZ racers, though it was rather less advanced, being designed purely for the street, not the track. It shared the SZ's 88in wheelbase, but not the racer's extensive use of aluminium – instead, the bodywork was made entirely of steel.

Not that the styling was without interest. The Kamm-tail rear end produced a short overhang, containing the Z's length and smoothing its passage through the atmosphere, while at the front the abruptly cut nose was covered by a Plexiglas sheet, the Alfa shield being cut within it and doubling as an air intake. Another novelty was the tailgate, which could be raised electrically by a few centimetres to improve ventilation, a feature it shared with the Lancia Fulvia Zagato.

But the steel bodywork, though a fraction lighter than the GT Junior's (2,024lb compared with the GT-J's 2,046lb) made for a heavier car than the SZ and TZ had been. So performance was not of the 'hold on to your headgear' kind, especially as the engine was the 89bhp twin-cam from the GT Junior. But the Z made up for its lack of go with

The Zagato-built Junior Z, launched in 1970, was originally based on Giulia 1300 running gear, but the car later received a 1600 engine, along with bigger bumpers and enlarged rear light clusters. This car is a 1300, however. The body was in steel rather than the aluminium Zagato usually favoured, leading to a minimal performance gain over an ordinary 1300 Junior. Only 1,510 Zs were made. ALFA ROMEO ARCHIVES

nimble handling – its running gear was all straight 105-series – and its lack of bulk, which is always an asset during a press-ahead drive.

It was a strict two-seater, but the room for the two in question and their luggage was generous, the boot area being particularly large. The interior design clearly was orientated to the business of driving and was kept as simple as possible. Most of the hardware came from the 105 parts catalogue, a ploy designed to keep down the price.

The Junior Z was first shown in November 1969 at the Turin show and it went on sale at the end of the following year. Production ended in 1972, by which time 1,108 cars had been built, and the 1300 was replaced by a 1600 version in November 1972.

Apart from its 109bhp 1,570cc engine, which raised the top speed to a rather more impressive 118mph, there were a few minor modifications to celebrate. The front bumper was beefed-up, the rear lamp clusters were enlarged to house reversing lamps, the two-spoke black-rimmed steering wheel was changed for a wooden three-

spoke item and the pedals were altered from the floor-mounted to the pendant variety. The weight of the Z climbed, too, by 66lb.

But despite its extra appeal, examples of the 1600 only trickled from the Zagato factory, and by the time production ended in 1975 the Z tally had only swollen by another 402 units. This makes it a rare car, and one that has often been overlooked by classic car collectors. One reason for this might be that it lacks the grace of the Giulia Sprint from which it was spawned, without offering any compensating on-the-road advantage. Rarity, its manners and the appeal of genuine, Zagato-built coachwork are its most appealing features.

ALFA ROMEO MONTREAL
The Montreal is not strictly a Giulia, although its floorpan and suspension were lifted straight from the GTV. When you realize that this meant a rigid axle had to deal with the 200bhp generated by a 2.6-litre V8 engine, you begin to understand

The Montreal, an expensive V8 coupe, was nevertheless based on a GTV floor. It was designed by Marcello Gandini when he was working for Bertone, and intended for display at the 1967 Canadian Expo rather than for production. But Alfa was persuaded to change its mind. ALFA ROMEO ARCHIVES

Three years later this was the result, more or less unchanged from the show car. It was powered by a 200bhp 2.6-litre V8 derived from the race 33, an output that tested the chassis somewhat. ALFA ROMEO ARCHIVES

A relatively short rear overhang hid the fact that the Montreal sat on a short wheelbase for such a large GT car, though those who attempted to enter the rear soon discovered the truth. The Montreal was produced from 1970 to 1977. ALFA ROMEO ARCHIVES

why the Montreal was something of a flawed design.

The car took its name from Expo '67, which was held in Montreal to celebrate the centenary of the federation of Canada. Alfa was commissioned to build a show car for the event, and the Montreal coupe was the result. It was designed by Bertone and used the V8 motor from the type 33 race car. It was so well received that Alfa was pressured into building it, and the production Montreal appeared three years later at the Geneva show in March 1970.

It was remarkably little changed from the show car (which now resides in the Alfa Romeo

museum at Arese) and it came with a five-speed gearbox, ventilated front brake discs, a limited-slip differential and the claim of a 140mph top speed. Unfortunately, power steering was not among the car's mechanical goodies, and the wheel was inordinately resistant at low speeds, nor was there much in the way of suspension modification to cope with the extra power apart from bigger 195/70-14in tyres. On the road, the Montreal was a disappointment compared with other exotic coupes of the day – it simply didn't have the grip and poise that a car of this class should be able to flaunt.

The ageing 105 chassis did more than place

limits on the Montreal's road qualities – it also undermined its packaging, the standard wheelbase being too short for a coupe of this size. Room in the rear was virtually non-existent, especially as the front seat backs almost touched the rear bench when a tall driver climbed aboard.

The compromised nature of the design was further underlined by the fact that the rear ride height had to be raised to minimize front-end lift at speed. Aerodynamics clearly had not been allowed to play much of a role in shaping the Montreal.

Despite all this, there was no denying that it was a dramatic-looking car, and a rapid one, too, capable of reaching 60mph in just over 8sec against the aural backdrop of metallic hammering made by what was really a race engine. Though the V8 was shrunk from its 3-litre racing capacity to 2.6 litres, the basic design remained

fundamentally intact. The engine was all-alloy with iron piston liners, and it used twin overhead camshafts per bank, hemispherical combustion chambers, Spica fuel injection, ram tubes tuned for length to optimize cylinder filling and electronic ignition.

It was a highly sophisticated engine and it tended to prove the point repeatedly by going wrong. Yet despite all its problems, and the fact that it lived through the energy crisis of the mid-Seventies, 3,925 Montreals were produced, taking Alfa back into a market it had not occupied since the old 2600 Sprint had died. That there was never a replacement probably says much about the company's experience during this little adventure. Only recently has there been any hint of a return to the prestige coupe market, and in the early Nineties Alfa seems to be treading quite tentatively towards that.

Look carefully and you can see the Giulia underpinnings, right down to the axle-locating T-bar at the rear. The V8 engine can be quite troublesome if not properly maintained, and there are few people who know how. ALFA ROMEO ARCHIVES

CHAPTER 11

A winning theme

It is amazing how selective history can be. Ask any enthusiast, in Britain at least, to name successful saloon race and rally cars of the Sixties and they'll doubtless mention names like Mini, Lotus Cortina, Escort, Porsche and perhaps even Citroen. But probably not Alfa, and less likely still Alfa GTA. Yet the GTA, the lightweight version of the GTV, was one of the most successful racers of all, collecting the European Touring Car Championship three times, in 1966, '67 and '68. And that represents barely half a shelf's worth of the multitude of trophies Alfas earned during the Sixties in the hands of works and private drivers.

The GTA was the descendant of the TZ, which itself had evolved from the SZ. Alfa Romeo had deserted the track in 1953, the Disco Volante cars being the last to officially represent the company. After that, competition was left in the hands of the privateers, though they occasionally received works support. But that did not mean that Alfas were not being raced successfully.

The SZ, a lightweight special based on the Giulietta, picked up class wins in endurance races at Monza, Sebring, Pescara, Daytona and in the Targa Florio, as well as in rallies, winning its class in the Alpine Cup three times in six years. The SZ's successor was the TZ, and with this new car came the establishment of Autodelta, Alfa's new racing arm, and the arrival of Carlo Chiti to run it.

Chiti was an aeronautics engineer who had started out in the experimental department at Alfa in 1952. He moved from there to Ferrari five years later to become the man behind the 2.5-litre

V6 Dino Formula One car, with which Mike Hawthorn won the 1958 World Championship, and the first mid-engined 1.5-litre Ferrari, the shark-nosed model with which Phil Hill became World Champion in 1961 and Ferrari took the Manufacturers' Championship. A dispute with Ferrari resulted in Chiti leaving in 1962 for an abortive season with the newly formed ATS Formula One team, an adventure which would leave him without work at the season's end.

At this point, Alfa recruited him to run Autodelta and develop the TZ. Work on this car had already been started by Satta and his engineering team, who used the new Giulia as the basis, though little apart from the engine and gearbox would be recognizable from the boxy little saloon. The TZ would effectively be an all-out racing version of the car, its aluminium Zagato body built around a spaceframe cage.

TZs first appeared in competition at the end of 1963, and instantly collected a class win in the FISA Cup race at Monza. Class, rather than outright wins, were the goal of Alfa's new weapon – it took far bigger and more expensive machinery to win outright – and the TZ duly picked up wins the following season at the Sebring 12-hour race, the Tour de France, the Targa Florio, the Nurburgring 1,000 Kilometres and at Le Mans. TZs also won the Coupe des Alpes and the Tour de Corse outright.

So Alfa's return to the track had been a success. It was not the same as winning the Formula One World Championship, of course, which Alfa had succeeded in doing in 1950 and 1951, but it was a return to racing and, perhaps more important commercially, with cars that at least bore some

Formula One racer Jochen Rindt and a GTA at the Sebring Four Hours race in 1966, which the pair won. The panel damage occurred during practice at the hands of another driver; the alloy outer panels rippled easily. ALFA ROMEO ARCHIVES

resemblance to the machinery on sale in showrooms, which certainly wasn't the case with an F1 car.

The next stage in the programme brought the similarity between road and track even closer. During 1965, the final part of the TZ programme was played out with the construction of 24 restyled cars, the TZ2s, a dozen of them in glassfibre, but for the following year Autodelta would switch to the new GTAs.

The reason for the shift of emphasis was a change in the rules of the European Touring Car Championship, which previously had stipulated that parts could be removed but not replaced. These restrictions were now relaxed to allow for more generous modifications, and it meant that the Giulia Sprint GT now offered promise as the basis of a racer, assuming its entrails could be altered to deliver the goods. From the promotional point of view this was good news because it made claims that Alfa raced the cars you could buy seem more believable, and it would also save money by avoiding the need to construct limited runs of entirely purpose-built machinery. And so the lightweight GTA 1600 was developed.

With its 170bhp twin-plug twin-cam motor the

GTA Corsa would prove a major challenger. Some private customers bought cars in 1965 while Autodelta was still campaigning the TZs, but for 1966 the team would enter the TZ2s in the GT class and the GTAs in the Touring category, which certainly kept Chiti and his crew busy.

The TZs did well on a limited front, but the GTAs enjoyed most of the victory spoils. Some of the more spectacular successes came at the hands of Jochen Rindt, who steered a GTA to victory in the Sebring 4-Hours race, disposing of 4.5-litre Dodge Darts and Plymouth Barracudas on the way, besides setting a new lap record. GTAs also came third, fourth and fifth in this race and, amazingly, Rindt's car won despite having been crashed in practice by another driver – it appeared on the grid looking like an entry for a banger race.

Andrea de Adamich and Teodoro Zeccoli won the Nurburgring 6-Hours race ahead of a pair of BMWs – a 2002 Ti and an 1800 Ti – but the real battle throughout that season was against the Lotus Cortinas driven by Sir John Whitmore and Jackie Stewart, among others. The Cortinas proved to be consistent winners of the early races, but then a GTA beat the Fords at Zandvoort and de Adamich won the 500-Kilometres European Championship race at Snetterton, these and other wins being sufficient to garner Alfa the European Touring Car Championship, while victories on the other side of the Atlantic gained the company the TransAm Championship against opposition from Lotus Cortinas, BMWs and Volvos.

So 1966 was a good year, with an amazing 200-plus victories scored in Alfas, but 1967 would be even better, the GTAs again winning the European Championship, in which 2-litre Porsche 911s now constituted the major opposition. Many of these races saw the GTAs picking up outright victories rather than class wins, and if they were defeated it was invariably by the larger-engined 911s.

This was also the year in which the formidably powerful GTA-SA racers were entered in some Group 6 races, the 220bhp machine achieving its first outright win at Hockenheim in the hands of the German driver S Dau. The following season the SAs took overall victories in the GP des Frontieres and the Coupe de Vitesse at Montlhéry, and there were successes at hillclimbs, too, as there were for the standard GTAs, which won the 1967 European Touring

Car Hillclimb Championship with Autodelta driver Ignazio Giunti at the wheel.

The Touring Car Championship went to Alfa yet again in 1968, GTAs also winning their class at the Daytona 24-Hours in Florida as well as various races in South Africa and Brazil. As if this was not enough, rivals were about to feel the full force of Alfa's competitive edge that year with the arrival of the GTA 1300s, which would be going for class wins in the lesser categories. In 1969 GTAs won the 1,300cc and 1,600cc classes in the European Challenge, which consisted of 10 long-distance races, and a GTA was also the car of the 1,600cc European Touring Car Champion Spartaco Dini. Underlining their versatility, GTAs would also win the European Rally Championship, which Autodelta had also found time to contest, the American SCCA Class C Championship, the Championship of Makes in Brazil and the Austrian Hillclimb Championship. It was not unusual for these Alfas to be winning events all over the world on the same day.

The 1300 GTAs continued to compete during 1970, but for the larger-capacity class Alfa relied on a competition version of the 1750 GTV, which had not long been launched, to win more

A squadron of GTAs on the banking at Monza, in Italy. Alfa's onslaught on the racing circuits was strong and highly effective – in its first season alone the GTA collected the Touring Car Championship in Europe and the TransAm Touring Car Championship in the US. And that was just the start. ALFA ROMEO ARCHIVES

A GTA on its way to second overall and first in class at the Spa-Francorchamps 24-hour race. There's extra lighting for the night drive and fatter tyres, but otherwise this car looks very standard. ALFA ROMEO ARCHIVES

trophies. This produced the fat-arched and potent GTAm racers, famed for cornering on three wheels, the inside front tyre dangling insouciantly as the coupes stormed to more wins. Dutchman Toine Hezemans won the European Touring Car Championship for Alfa again in 1970, claiming victories at Monza, Zandvoort, Budapest, Brno and Jarama on the way, and he won his class the following year when a 3-litre Capri won the championship outright. Ford's victory in 1971 marked the beginning of the end of the GTA's domination of the series as bigger-engined machinery, notably the Capri RS2600s, took a turn at the top.

But GTAs and GTAms were not the only cars to win laurels for Alfa. Plenty of people were competing with the production GTV, and a number of class wins were won with them in Australia and elsewhere, and even the Spider won trophies, winning the Cesana-Sestriere hillclimb in Italy and the National Championship at Austin, Texas. Duettos fitted with the twin-plug head, which gave the car a top speed of 133mph,

achieved class wins in the Targa Florio and the Circuit of Mugello.

The Sixties brought Alfa Romeo literally hundreds of victories, many of them with derivatives of the Giulias, during what many would argue was Alfa's most successful postwar era, in both production and racing terms. So many victories did an enormous amount to boost the company's credibility and win it a place in the hearts of thousands of enthusiasts. The considerable investment in competition activities paid off well, both then and, through its legacy of success, in more recent years when the company has been close to extinction amid a morass of bad planning, fields of unwanted cars, huge losses and terrifying labour problems. The dedicated enthusiasts, the ones who remember Alfa's past victories and successes and love the firm for it, have done much to keep a flame alive during the bad times.

Alfa's racing successes have not only been at the top level, either – the qualities inherent in the cars have made them the choice of dozens of

The GTA in its characteristic wheel-cocking attitude, brought about by the lower wishbone extensions they wore to produce negative camber. This is Nanni Galli at Vienna in 1967. ALFA ROMEO ARCHIVES

Toine Hezemans in a 1750 GTAm at the Brno Grand Prix in 1970, which he went on to win, seen here in spectacular wheel-dangling style. He also won the European Touring Car Championship that year. Note the fat wheelarch fairings and the generous rubber. ALFA ROMEO ARCHIVES

The Spider was raced and rallied far less frequently than the GT, but it collected some silverware none the less. This 1750 is contesting the 1971 Coupe des Alpes and heading for first in the Group 3 category. ALFA ROMEO ARCHIVES

Alfa Romeos are enormously popular race cars at all levels – this Spider is contesting the Slick 50 budget road saloon race series. ALFA ROMEO ARCHIVES

amateur racers who get a kick from wearing out rubber most weekends in the various club championships.

It is for reasons such as this that the Alfa Romeo marque name is still so well regarded and seen as an exotic, prestigious and sporting brand, despite its disasters. Here is the real proof that racing (and winning) pays.

CHAPTER 12

Beware oil and rust
How to buy and what to look for

As I write this, it is still possible to buy an Alfa Spider new. It may look different from the original 1966 Duetto, but mechanically it is much the same car. In Britain it is supplied fitted with a three-way catalyst, a removable hardtop and left-hand drive, though an approved RHD conversion, reputedly of high quality, is offered by a company called Seaking. Another source is the Surrey-based dealers Bell and Colvill, who have been importing and converting Spiders for many years.

Inevitably, buying a secondhand example of either model, Spider or GTV, is considerably cheaper, at least in terms of initial outlay. Both cars are readily available after a hunt, though rust has meant a high attrition rate in Britain, many coupes in particular meeting an early death at the crushers. Spiders tend to live longer because they are more likely to be coveted.

The best sources are via the classic car magazines, which invariably have plenty of Spiders and a few coupes for sale, as well as *Exchange and Mart* and the various regional *Trader* magazines, although sightings in these are much rarer. Another good source is the Alfa Romeo Owners Club magazine, which always has a selection of cars for sale, and at least as important, a stack of spares advertised by members.

The club is worth joining for this alone, though it offers much more than this professionally produced magazine, including an excellent racing series, the grand-scale National Alfa Day at Stanford Hall, in Leicestershire (a jamboree of cars, spares and socializing), and a smattering of technical advice in the magazine, although it is a bit weak in this area. There are also local sections of the club, enabling Alfisti to get their monthly fix of Alfa chatter nearer to home.

There are two major considerations when buying anything other than the more recent, post-1983 Spiders. First, corrosion can make an awful mess of these cars and cost a lot to fix, and second, some spares are extremely difficult to locate and costly to buy, particularly body panels.

Alfa GB, for example, carries virtually nothing in stock for the coupes and pre-1983 Spiders other than the more obvious service items, and the Alfa factory in Milan does not have a great deal more. However, it is sometimes worth trying to place an order because there is always a slender chance of Milan having the part required, in which case Alfa's UK arm can obtain it for you. Generally, however, it is usually more beneficial to try the non-franchised specialists, amongst the most prominent in the UK being EB Spares, in Wiltshire. This company does an excellent job of catering for these cars, but here again there are dozens of items which they are unable to supply.

The most difficult to obtain spares are those concerned with trim and bodywork. It is easier to find panels for the Spider because some of them remain in production – the doors and bonnet, for example – but obtaining a bootlid for a Duetto is out of the question. Lights, bumpers, trim strips and many other little knick-knacks are also rare.

Matters are even worse for the coupes because they have been out of production for so long. Body panels can only be found after a committed search, and the same applies with lamp assemblies, petrol tanks, badges, bumpers and masses of detail items. Perseverance pays, however, and so does settling for secondhand items which can

Scene from a National Alfa Day, held at Stanford Hall, in the UK. Hundreds of Alfisti converge on the day, bringing much appealing machinery and the chance to chat about Alfas all day without excuse. Alfa owners clubs tend to be well subscribed, very active and well worth joining. ALFA ROMEO OWNERS CLUB

occasionally be found in good condition.

Interior trim for both cars, including seats, carpets and door casings, disappeared from the factory stores long ago, but there are specialist suppliers, Coburns being among the best known, which can supply good-quality reproduction parts, often using the original material. The same company also offers hoods for Spiders. Bear in mind, though, that a full trim set can cost a fortune.

The good news is that mechanical components are easy to find, first because the Spider is still in production, and second because the twin-cam engines still play a major part in the modern Alfa Romeo range. There is very little which is not available, and a search will usually turn up the more difficult parts. Items that may well prove elusive, perhaps close to impossible to obtain, will be the obscure ones such as the kit for the Dunlop brakes of the early coupes, or pieces unique to some of the specials such as the GTA and SS. These cars are very different, very rare, and cost a fortune, so before buying one it is important to take professional advice because paying for a duffer could prove to be a very costly exercise. Meanwhile, this chapter will concentrate

on the mainstream coupes and Spiders.

Because mechanical spares are easy to locate (and the mechanical units are relatively easy to fix), buying advice is quite simple. Choose the most rot-free example you can and then make sure that the car's interior is fundamentally sound. Worry less about the mechanical condition, but when things do go wrong, as inevitably they will from time to time, bear in mind the following guidance. As the Spider and coupe are identical mechanically, the comments apply to both models.

ENGINE

It is the heart of the car, yet in many respects the Alfa twin-cam is the component you least need to worry about because it is strong and easily repaired. A well-maintained example can prove reliable for 150,000 miles if its cylinder-head bolts have been torqued regularly. Even abused engines will reach 80,000 miles without major calamity, though by then they will be far from at their best.

Maintenance is the key. Regular fresh oil and a filter change count for a lot, as does anti-freeze.

This GTV might look past it, but its core structure will almost certainly be sound. If large sections of the floor and the chassis longitudinals are corroded, the car is probably beyond saving. This one has suffered in the typical areas – rear wheel-arches, both inner and outer, the rear valance and under the chrome strip of the rear side window. MIKE BROWN

The same car, after surgery on the offside. The wheel-arch is available as a repair section, but the rear valance was made up, though this, too, is now available. The bootlid has been removed for attention to its trailing edge, which is another rust-prone zone. MIKE BROWN

The twin-cam is an all-alloy unit and without the corrosion-inhibiting properties of anti-freeze the waterways can corrode, which is something that is hard to detect. Cracked blocks and cylinder-heads are the other potential consequences of using tap water for coolant. The block is the more likely to suffer, being a weaker structure, and there are no core plugs to blow first. Cracks are most likely to be found around the oil pressure sensor aft of the carburettors, which is fairly easy to spot, and in the water chambers behind the timing gear under the front cover, which is not. If the head cracks it will most likely be around the spark plug holes.

Much cheaper to fix is a blown head gasket, a more common ailment of the 2-litre engine, which had the least amount of metal around its bores. Look on the exhaust side for a trio of oily weeps beneath the manifold signalling a gasket in decline. Some leakage is acceptable, but the head will have to come off eventually. Oil can also seep from the front seal, so look for a single trail at the front of the sump. It is not serious, but it will be

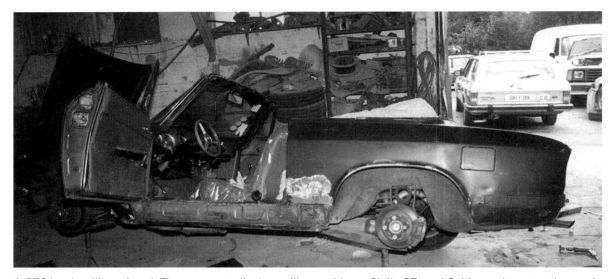

A GTC has its sills replaced. There are actually three sills per side on Giulia GTs and Spiders – the outer, the one in the middle and the inner sill, and the middle sill is visible here; in this instance it is largely intact, which is not always the case. Outer sill replacement is a fiddly job on these cars – genuine panels require that the base of the front and rear wings be pulled back to allow the new panel to be tucked underneath. Pattern sills that merely run the length of the doors are not good enough because they fail to replace the missing strength. It is important to check that the new sill bows in order to follow the curvature of the car's flank – not all replacements do. MIKE BROWN

messy. Very early Giulia Sprints did without an extra pair of cam box bolts at the front of the engine, and oil can spread from here, too, but again this is nothing serious.

Oil pressure itself varies enormously, not because of poor engine build quality, but because the gauges had low-grade internals. Look instead for a brisk reaction from the needle once the engine has started, and not too much variation as the revs rise and fall. Low pressure when the engine is hot and idling should not be a concern, though, nor should some oil consumption as all twin-cams use a little, even when young.

In any case, big-end failure is virtually unheard-of on these engines, especially the 1300s. More likely is the need for a rebore, which is relatively easy to administer because of the linered construction. A set of pistons, rings and liners is not cheap, but it will certainly rejuvenate a high-mileage engine.

The cylinder-head and cams are unlikely to need serious work with age. Clattery tappets indicate the need for reshimming, though earlier engines tended to be noisier anyway. The timing gear can be a source of mild trouble, though. A clatter at 2,200rpm indicates the need to retension the timing chain, which in principle is quite easy. However, the specialist advice is not to follow the instructions of the manuals, which suggest adjustment while the engine is running.

The reason is that the timing adjuster assembly is likely to be missing some of its internals if the car is old, and if tampered with this could lead to valves hitting pistons. It is better to check all this while the engine is static and verify the correct cam timing at the same time. Incorrect cam timing has a severe effect on performance and is usually the reason for a lack of go.

Dirty air filters, which are surprisingly commonplace, do not help, either. The carburettor mounting rubbers, which are surprisingly expensive to replace, can also affect running. Check for air leaks by grasping the carbs when the engine is running and moving them about. If this affects the idle, then there's a problem. The carburettors should also be mounted at the correct angle, that is tilted slightly towards the engine so that fuel flows towards the ports naturally. If they tilt the wrong way fuel can run into the air filter at idle and produce petrol fumes. Adjustment via the support rod is fairly easy.

Alfa used three suppliers of carburettors – Weber, Dellorto and Solex – all of which deliver much the same performance in practice. But the Solex carbs have been known to give trouble because their spindles turn directly in the bodies rather than in the roller bearings used by the other makes. Eventually, the bodies wear, which can cause air leaks that make the spindles chatter and the idle speed vary.

Despite its sophistication, the twin-cam engine is remarkably robust, though regular oil changes help, as does a healthy dose of corrosion-inhibiting anti-freeze. Likely ailments as the miles climb are a rattling timing chain, head gasket failure (particularly on the 2-litres) and general wear of bearing surfaces. The twin carbs require specialist attention to set up, but they stay in tune well. TIM WREN

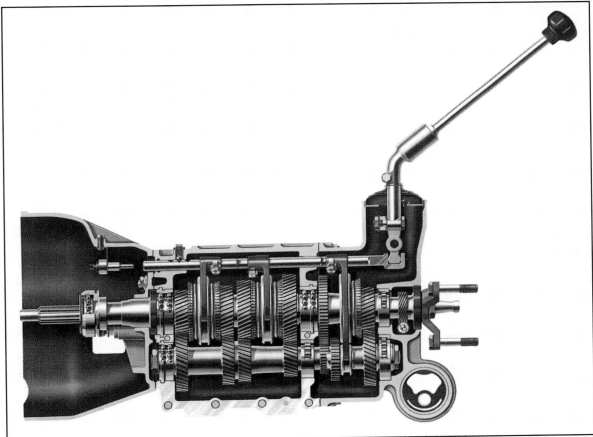

Second-gear synchromesh is the weakest element of the transmission, wearing when the gearbox oil is cold. Oil can leak through the gaiter at the top of the box, where the gear-lever enters, because it is often split or unsecured. Poor gear selection is rare, but sometimes caused by an incorrectly located centre console. The clutch is quite robust on later cars, but the rubber at the joint between the propshaft and the gearbox can disappear on all models, generating noise, as does a worn propshaft centre steady.

The front crossmember below the radiator is prone to rot, as is the front valance, which has been cut away here. Front anti-rollbar mounts can also fail. None of these repairs is difficult for a competent welder. The spring pans, against which the axle stands are butting in this shot, can also rot through, allowing the coils to break free – something worth checking for. MIKE BROWN

Water pumps tend to last well if anti-freeze is present and the cooling system is generally bug-free. Some specialists recommend the removal of the fan shroud, which is meant to improve cooling in hot weather at idle. In practice its presence makes little difference (both Spider and GTV tend to run cool, anyway), but merely increases the chance of a holed radiator because the fan's plastic blades are brittle and if one snaps off the shrouding will direct it straight through the core.

The best measure of engine condition is to drive the car and listen hard. If it is rough and listless, then work is needed. But these are not particularly difficult engines to repair, despite the additional complexity of twin camshafts, nor do they need a multitude of special tools in order to administer a fix.

TRANSMISSION

The Giulia's five-speed gearbox is most unlikely to give up completely, but synchromesh wear, particularly on second and to a lesser extent third gear, is a problem. Crunching into second gear when the car is cold is the all-too-obvious symptom. A cheap(er) repair can be effected by swapping the fifth gear synchro cones for second gear's and fourth's with third's, but this is not ideal. New cones tend to be pricey, though. Jumping out of reverse, caused by bent selector forks, is a rare problem. Apart from that there is little else to report.

The clutches of the 2000s are very robust, those of the earlier models being a little less durable.

The split upper wishbone can cause clonking noises when its joints are worn. Note the severe corrosion of the inner wing here – it is repairable, but expensive. MIKE BROWN

Very early Sprints used a VW Beetle-style clutch that could be adjusted for wear once out of the car, but the exercise is barely worthwhile. Early models had a cable clutch. The cable rarely snaps, but it does allow some vibration through the pedal. The hydraulic systems of later models only give trouble if the car is left for a long time, in which case the slave seals can blow out.

The propshaft has a pair of UJs and it is not uncommon for one of them to need replacing. A vibrating rumble heard through the transmission tunnel is the giveaway, as is clunking under acceleration and deceleration.

Differentials are just as robust. There is always some backlash, and they usually weep oil, but neither of these imperfections is worth worrying

Minor ailments tend to afflict the rear suspension. The trailing arm itself rarely corrodes seriously, but its bushes wear and the straps preventing the axle dropping too far can snap, while the rubber bump stop – the collar above the brake disc – can drop off; replacement is usually difficult. Springs sag with age, though dampers rarely fail; Konis are widely considered the best replacement. Brakes can give trouble if they are the early Dunlop variety; the main problem on later cars is bleeding the twin-servo system fitted to right-hand-drive models. MIKE BROWN

about. A limited-slip differential was an option on 1750s and early 2000s before becoming standardized, but the only sure way to tell if your car has one is to remove the diff filler plug and take a peek inside. If you can see a cylinder it has one, otherwise the planetary gears will be on view. If the slippery diff works, it should be possible to leave a pair of black tyre trails of equal length on the tarmac after a fast start.

SUSPENSION

As with most cars, the main problems here tend to be associated with bearings and bushes. Shock absorbers rarely give up completely, but merely turn soft instead. Generally the car should feel taut and responsive. If it doesn't, then you have evidence that it has been driven hard and possibly even abused.

A rear end that self-steers is good evidence of this. Check by accelerating quite briskly on a smooth, level road, then back off the throttle. If the car steers in one direction and then the other the quartet of trailing arm bushes are worn. They are not too expensive to replace, though they are difficult to extract. Wear in this area is a good guide to the sort of life the car has led. If it self-steers it has either been driven hard or it has covered a lot of miles.

Less likely is wear in the bushes that locate the T-piece that restrains the rear axle. Tired bushes

here allow some axle movement, but changing them is not difficult. Further trouble spots at the rear end include broken rebound straps and missing rubber bump stops, though these are minor ailments. Removing the bump stop mounting plates is not easy, though, because they are often rusted solid.

Up front, troubles can be more serious. A mild clunking noise under braking is probably the top nylon castor bush, a more severe knock the forward bush on the same arm. The top and bottom balljoints can suffer some wear without much consequence, which is just as well because it is hard to detect merely by grabbing the wheel and rocking it when the car is on the ground. If there is a noise from the front end over bumps it is likely to be a wishbone bush, which is more difficult to change. This failure is more common on pre-1965 Sprints, which lacked a dust cap over the forward bush and consequently allowed dirt to enter.

These cars also have lower wishbone mountings with only two 22mm retaining bolts, whereas later models have four 17mm fixings. The reason for the change was that stress cracks could develop around the mountings of the earlier cars, and in extreme cases the wishbones could wrench free. Checking for these cracks is not easy, even when the car is on a ramp, but obviously it is worth making the effort. Minor cracking is not too much of a problem because it can be welded-up, but anything more severe is going to be very expensive to remedy. The Spider does not suffer from any of the wishbone mounting problems because it came out a year after the modifications had been introduced.

Spring pans also need to be examined – they retain the lower end of the coil – because they can corrode, eventually allowing the spring to break through the pan, past the triangular wishbone and on to the ground. Having experienced this on my own car I can tell you that the results are fairly spectacular, as some gouge marks around the Kingston one-way system southwest of London once testified. Luckily, this malady tends to strike at very low speed and leaves the driver with some control of the car. Checking the pans is not easy, though, because from underneath they tend to look fine, the corrosion usually starting above where water collects if the drain holes become blocked. Matters are not helped by the alloy shims used to correct the ride height, and which prompt electrolytic corrosion. The only good news is that the problem is rare and cheap to fix.

Another front suspension problem is corrosion of the forward anti-roll bar mountings, which bolt into the front crossmember. Eventually the bar can break free, though this occurrence is not dangerous, just costly.

Wheel bearings rarely give trouble at the front because they are so large, but the rear set can wear. They are easy to change, though. The steering gear, of which there are two types, is reliable, but the steering box occasionally needs topping up, and if the idler becomes dry, play in the system may prompt failure of the annual MoT test.

Despite this long list of ailments, the 105-series suspension is pretty tough and dependable. But it does pay to check because these are enthusiasts' cars and one can assume that they have been subjected to higher than average stresses.

BRAKES

Three types of braking system have been fitted to these cars. The first, a Dunlop system, was used

An example of the severe bodging these cars can suffer. This Duetto has bad structural corrosion and the front of the sills are missing completely; they have been replaced here by pounds of filler and bits of alloy sheet. MIKE BROWN

A Spider front wing is a large panel and can hide much trouble beneath. This car is not too bad, but the forward edge of the sill, exposed to mud flung up by the wheel, has corroded. MIKE BROWN

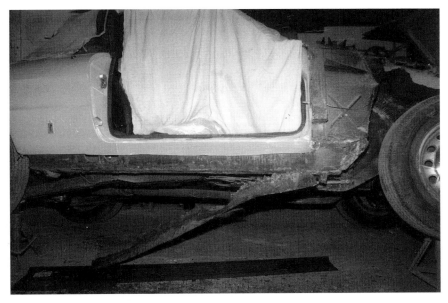

The same car minus the outer sill and revealing the middle sill that has also begun to rust. The sills are structurally extremely important to the Spider because the car is open-topped. Only one side should be removed at a time, otherwise the body can bow. MIKE BROWN

only on the early Sprints, and is generally reckoned to be sufficiently troublesome to warrant changing for the later Ate system, which proved to be more reliable. This was a single-circuit layout; in 1970 both the 1750 Spider and the 1750 GTV (the Mk 2 version) came with dual-circuit brakes, necessitating twin servoes for right-hand-drive cars.

The Dunlop system was a very early disc brake design (few volume-produced cars had discs in the early Sixties, remember) that used dual-piston Jaguar calipers. Because the pistons were prone to seizing, uneven braking was frequently a problem, as was the handbrake, the mechanical efficiency of which was so poor that it rarely worked at all. Ate-braked cars were given a redesigned handbrake that operates on drums machined into the rear discs. The pads rarely wear out, which is a comfort because removing the rear discs for an inspection is not easy. Handbrake cables can chafe around their mounting on the offside trailing arm, and the ratchet can fail, sometimes because it is loose rather than worn.

Failure of the master-cylinder is a more frequent problem with these cars than with most because it is bolted under the floor where it is exposed to water and dirt, the corollary of the floor-hinged pedals fitted to all right-hand-drive coupes and most RHD Spiders. Replacements are not always available because they are now batch-manufactured, so laying one down (in a dry place) for future use is a sensible idea. The brake light switch often fails, so replacing it with a better-made one from a Mini,

which screws straight in, is also a good move, Brake pipe corrosion, particularly around the cylinder, can also be a problem.

Servoes can also leak internally, which is expensive if both go. The main problem with dual-circuit brakes is bleeding them, however. Success is only guaranteed if one front and one rear wheel are bled simultaneously, with the engine running to scavenge the servoes.

ELECTRICS
Despite the appalling reputation of Italian electrical componentry, most problems in this area tend to stem either from poor earth connections in the case of a lighting failure, or dirty connections in the fuse box. Failure of the part itself is rare. However, the Bosch starters and generators used on later cars do tend to be more dependable. More important, though, is a healthy battery as these cars require quite a kick to turn over, especially when cold.

MISCELLANEOUS ITEMS
❏ Exhaust. Not a problem because replacements are easy to obtain. It is essential to hang the pipework correctly, however, to allow for movement when the engine rocks under its own torque. It is also worth knowing that the exhaust manifold to cylinder-head gaskets can easily be fitted upside-down, and if this happens gas flow and performance will be restricted. In the case of

The Spider's nose-section is vulnerable to parking damage because it is so low, and usually needs work. Like the GTV's, the front crossmember below the radiator rots. This car also has rusty headlamp bowls, a typical small problem. MIKE BROWN

the coupe, persistent exhaust smells in the cabin are often caused by an ineffective boot seal allowing fumes to be sucked forwards into the car. A new rubber is the only answer.

❑ Engine mountings. These can break, the rubber shearing from the steel mount, which is hard to detect. However, excessive lateral movement of the gearlever is a clue. In extreme cases it can knock the headlamp stalk from main beam to dip when the lever is in the fifth-gear position. The metal part of the mountings can also break, but you will probably hear this.

❑ Heater. This can give up if the diaphragm in the tap swells up, blocking off the hot water supply. On early cars changing the rubber is possible, but later models had a sealed unit. It is fiddly, but not expensive, to mend.

If a long list like this puts you off, it shouldn't. Going into this much detail can give the impression that these cars are prone to a

disturbingly broad range of ailments. In fact, the 105-series cars are basically very reliable. They are not especially complex, and though the engine has quite an exotic specification it was sufficiently well developed by 1963, when the Giulia Sprint was launched, to have had most trouble spots exorcized. If one of these Alfas is unreliable it will almost certainly be because it has been neglected.

Unfortunately, the fact that these cars can take a lot of abuse and still run strongly encourages some people to ignore maintenance. Rectifying the results of this will ultimately prove costly, but probably not as expensive as repairing a rotten body. The following is a guide to what can rust.

BODYWORK

Like many cars from the Sixties which have been imported from warmer climes, the Spider and Giulia coupe can rust prodigiously because their undersides simply had inadequate defence against Britain's and other more northern countries' lethal combination of salt, mud and moisture. In fact, they were probably no worse than a lot of Fords, Vauxhalls and similar locally produced cars of the period, but the reputation for rusting has stuck.

The good news in this respect is that these Alfas can look terrible, yet prove to be salvageable because their basic structure has remained sound. It is a question of determining what is economic to repair (and as these cars become rarer and more desirable the equation tends to change) or how badly one wants to save the car in question.

Though the two models share certain structural elements, hardtop and open-top structures inevitably differ in many respects and it is therefore sensible to describe their problem areas separately.

GIULIA SPRINT GT, GT JUNIOR, GTV

Although there are some body-in-white differences between early and late coupes, particularly around the front end, there is not much difference in the way they decay. The most vulnerable areas are the rear wheelarches, the bottoms of the doors, the sills, the front crossmember (to which the anti-roll bar bolts), the spare wheel well and the recess in which the fuel tank is seated. The floor can also become holed around the pedal area.

None of these problems is insurmountable, but sill repairs are more complex than they might seem because there are actually three sills on each side of the car – an outer one, the one in the middle which cannot be seen until the outer one has been peeled away, and the inner one, which is visible from inside the car. The sills contribute much to the coupe's strength, not least because

A boat-tail Spider approaching the priming stage, having had new sills, front wings, valances and door bottoms, all typical corrosion zones for these cars. Floors are also vulnerable in the Spider because hoods leak, especially in old age. MIKE BROWN

effectively the car has no upper B-pillar. Replacing the outer sill calls for peeling away the base of the front and rear wings so that the ends of the new panel can be slid into position beneath them. This is a detail which some repairers and bodgers fail to take into account, especially if they buy pattern sills which are not shaped to run under the wings. Before this stage is reached it is likely that the middle sill will also need attention, although the inner one may well be intact (if this one is also rotten the car has probably gone too far unless the rest of it is particularly good).

Replacing the rear wheelarches is easy enough (good pattern replacements are available), as is repairing the front crossmember once the radiator has been removed. Front wings are more difficult because replacements are almost impossible to find, making patched repairs a necessity. They tend to go at the base, behind the front wheel, along a vertical stretch where the forward dust shield butts against them, and sometimes they go at the top rear, next to the doors, where it is harder to rectify them. Filler in all of these areas is a strong possibility in anything other than an immaculate example.

The spare wheel well is a straightforward repair or replacement task, and if a new well is unavailable, the well from a Ford Cortina estate is almost identical and certainly cheaper. Repairs to the fuel tank mounting flange can be more difficult, and the tank will probably also need replacing. Corrosion is usually caused by a leaking bootlid or by a perished fuel filler rubber.

Doors tend to rot along the bottom, around the door handle apertures, and at the top, beneath the chrome strip. Good secondhand examples can

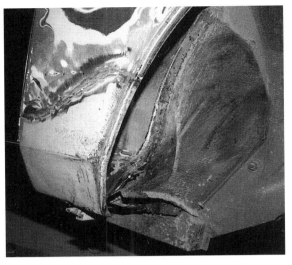

Detail of the trailing edge of a GTV front wing, repaired with a replacement section that some specialists can now offer. The same part is available for the Spider. This car also needs attention to the inner wing, which is holed, though this is more rare. The box-section visible at the bottom is actually a thin metal shield for the brake master-cylinder, but it protects it only to a limited extent. MIKE BROWN

sometimes be found, but new doors are no longer available. The bonnet very rarely corrodes, but the bootlid can decay along the trailing edge. Headlamp holders also rust, as do the lamp reflectors (this is sometimes called Carello disease) and finding replacements can be difficult.

Repairing the floor around the pedals should not be too difficult unless the brake and clutch master-cylinders have to be removed. The floor is unlikely to corrode unless water leaks into the cabin regularly.

Post-restoration assembly is surprisingly time-consuming if the details are to be attended to properly. New headlamp bowls are not available, so they must be derusted and thoroughly protected before re-assembly. The lamps themselves are also corrosion-prone, though replacements are available, at a price.

Spare wheel wells in both Spider and GTV rust out, mainly because condensation collects there, along with dirt; the spare grinds the dirt into the paint as the car travels along, until there's no protection at all. New wells are available, but they are not cheap. TIM WREN

Rust can also develop under the screen rubbers, especially on the SE, the vinyl roof of which is nailed into position – an amazing fixing arrangement (amazingly stupid, that is). Rot can spread under the vinyl undetected, leaving holes in the B-pillars in bad cases. The metal around the base of the rear screen may also need changing, but this section can sometimes be cut from another unaffected example.

A coupe can be rotten in all of the areas mentioned above and still be repaired, if expensively. But if the car has rotted around the longitudinal members to which the suspension is mounted, this can be terminal, as can extensive surface rusting underneath. These are strong cars, though, and if the core body is sound it can be repaired to a high standard.

SPIDER

The cars suffer the same sill and rear wheelarch troubles as the coupes, and the sills are just as difficult to replace. Doors, however, are not as prone to deterioration as those of the coupes – they usually rot at the base only – and bonnets tend not to rust, but as with the coupe the trailing edge of the boot is vulnerable.

So is the spare wheel well and the front crossmember, as well as the front valance. Additional problems are caused mainly by water leaking into the cabin, which is a strong possibility even from new because the hoods are rarely completely leak-proof. In bad cases the underlay becomes wet, speeding corrosion of the floor and footwells from the inside out. It pays to remove the carpets and dry out the cabin regularly.

Door bottoms are more vulnerable on the GTV than on the Spider, though they rot in both cases. You can obtain new Spider doors, but none are available for the GTV. TIM WREN

The interior will be easy to strip down, but not to re-assemble. It is best to label every item and keep it with its fixings. Most cabin fittings are very difficult to obtain, which is something to bear in mind when contemplating buying a car. TIM WREN

Because it is an open car, the Spider has a lot of additional strengthening which needs to be checked. There is some quite complex panelling inside the rear of the front wings (which is hidden by a dust shield) and at the forward end of the inner rear wings. The inner rear wheelarches are also susceptible to rot.

If sill replacement is necessary it is crucial that only one side is repaired at a time. As the Spider has no roof, unless it is properly supported, the body will promptly emulate a banana if both sills are removed simultaneously.

Although some panels for the Spider, particularly the boat-tail models, are no longer obtainable, the good news is that most of the core metalwork is available because the car remains in production.

A 1975 2000 GTV and a lonely Welsh mountain road –
all you need for a wonderful drive. MERVYN
FRANKLYN

The Giulietta Sprint appeared in 1954, though this is a later example from the 101 series, identified by the mesh side grilles. ALFA ROMEO ARCHIVES

The original wooden Giulietta styling buck, template for the steel prototypes. ALFA ROMEO ARCHIVES

Giuliettas made great race cars thanks to a well-sorted, if roll-prone chassis and the tuning potential of the twin-cam engine. ALFA ROMEO OWNERS CLUB

A Giulia Spider 1600 at speed. Essentially it was identical to the earlier Giulietta Spider, distinguished mainly by the bonnet's dummy air scoop. ALFA ROMEO OWNERS CLUB

The 1,570cc, 92bhp version of the twin-cam, as fitted to the Giulia Sprint and Spider. Apart from the breathing arrangements, it looks largely the same in the 1992 Spider. TIM WREN

Right: The 1962 Giulia saloon, first of the 105 series that spawned the Spider and Giulia Sprint GT. It may not have looked a beauty, but it was roomy, refined, brisk and it handled well. TIM WREN

Left: The almost outlandish Sprint Speciale, a highly aerodynamic coupe built first on Giulietta and later on Giulia mechanicals.

The TZ, for Tubolare Zagato, was Alfa's highly specialized and immensely successful competition weapon of the early Sixties. Much that was learnt from it would be embodied in the Giulia series. ALFA ROMEO ARCHIVES

Below: The engine that powered the Giulia, the 1,570cc twin-cam. Note the all-alloy construction, even down to the finned oil sump. Five main bearings, wet-linered pistons and the duplex timing chain all helped the engine towards its reputation for durability. Note also the carbs (only one is shown) bolted direct to the head, helping the excellent throttle response. ALFA ROMEO ARCHIVES

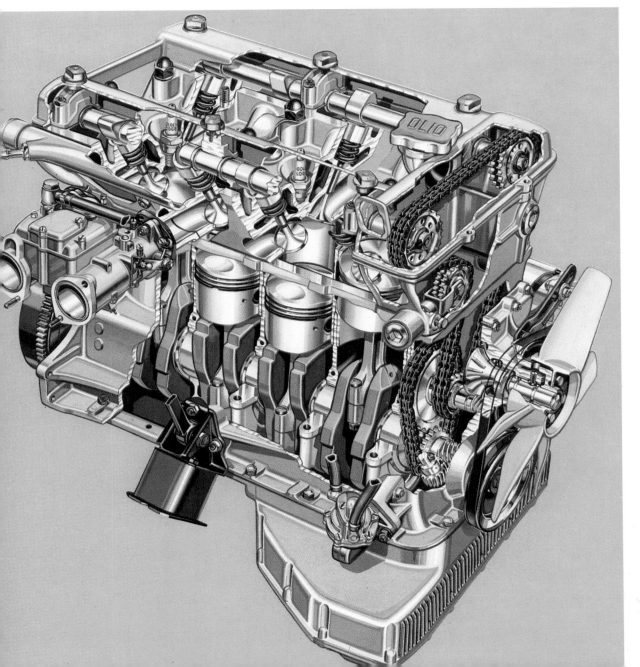

Giorgetto Giugiaro's rendering for the 1963 Giulia Sprint GT, which he designed for Bertone while on national service. ITALDESIGN

The car itself – a 1963 Giulia Sprint GT. There was minimal transformation from paper to metal. ITALDESIGN

The Giulia Sprint's 106bhp twin-cam. The air cleaner was mounted remote from the carbs to allow for a lower bonnet line. TIM WREN

The Sprint GT's dash was relatively simple and less elegant than the car itself. Instrumentation was very complete, though it didn't look it. TIM WREN

The Giulia GTC, a Sprint with its top lopped off. An elegant 2+2 converted by coachbuilders Touring, it did not prove a great success. This right-hand-drive car is one of only 99 built. TIM WREN

The Pininfarina-styled Spider emerged in 1966 after a long gestation to mixed reviews. Pininfarina developed the style quite publicly, revealing a number of prototypes on the way. PININFARINA

One of the earlier developments was the 1960 3500SS Coupe Super Sport Speciale, better known as the Tre S, which shared the Spider's plan-form, as well as its front wings and their Perspex lamp covers. PININFARINA

The 1961 Giulietta Spider Speciale Aerodinamica was much closer to the final car, differing only in having pop-up headlamps, slimmer bumpers and different roofing arrangements. PININFARINA

The 1966 1600 Spider, likened to a cuttlefish bone and a lentil seed by the doubters, but a coveted car today. The scallop in its flanks was a particularly contentious feature. TIM WREN

The Spider's cabin was simple but well equipped, housing a pair of comfortable reclining seats, a painted facia housing plenty of instruments, and refinements such as wind-up windows and face-level ventilation. TIM WREN

The Giulia 1600 GTA, a race special that resembled the standard GT but had lightweight alloy body panels and twin-spark plug cylinder head. TIM WREN

Class of '66. Clockwise, the 1600 Duetto, GTA, Giulia saloon and GTC. The 105-series range had proliferated enormously in the four years since the saloon's launch, with plenty still to come. TIM WREN

The Kamm-tail Spider ran more or less unchanged from 1970 to 1983, housing first the 1750 engine and, from 1971, the 2000. JOHN MASON

The 1300 GTA, launched in 1968, was much the same as the more potent 1600, but featured dramatic decals, including a large serpent on the bonnet. TIM WREN

The Mark 2 GT Junior dash was essentially as the 1750 GTV's, but lacking the pricier model's wood centre console. The speedo and rev-counter were unusually large. ALFA ROMEO ARCHIVES

The rare Alfa Junior Z, built by Zagato and launched in 1970, was a distant successor to the SZ and TZ, but was not as light, being steel rather than aluminium-bodied, which made for minimal weight saving over the standard Junior. CAR MAGAZINE

A Montreal at speed during the launch of the car at Alfa's Balocco test track in 1970. It was fast, being V8-powered, but was under-mined by a chassis that fell far short of the promise of its supercar looks. CAR MAGAZINE

A 1975 example of the 2000 GTV, which looked virtually identical to the previous 1750 save for a new grille. Though dated in many respects, the Giulia coupe aged well and remained attractive even at its demise in 1976. MERVYN FRANKLYN

The GTV's dash changed when it became a 2000, and though ergonomically it was not much improved, it still looked classy, not least because of the wood-rimmed steering wheel. MERVYN FRANKLYN

Interior of a 1978 US-spec Spider, which barely differed from the European version. This was probably the best interior, combining many detail refinements with the most attractive dash layout. PININFARINA

The 1974 Spider Aerodinamica, a design exercise by Pininfarina, presaged the 1983 facelift, which included the front and rear spoilers, though not, thankfully, the paint scheme. PININFARINA

The 1983 facelift brought the Spider new bumpers, a new grille, as well as spoilers front and rear, to create the least attractive look, save for the QV model. PININFARINA

The 1986 Quadrifoglio Verde Spider, a top-of-the-range model that came with particularly ugly skirts and spoilers and new alloy wheels. The hardtop was new, too, and lives on unchanged for the 1992 model.

The 1992 Spider looks much tidier than the previous version, the body-colour bumpers and sill extensions blending far more successfully than before. MERVYN FRANKLYN

It may be dated, but it still has style and class, and is just as irresistible on a winding, empty road. MERVYN FRANKLYN

APPENDIX A

US specification variations

Although it has never sold huge numbers of cars in the United States, Alfa Romeo has been dependent on the American market as a major source of sales for many of its more specialized cars, none more so than the Spider, a car almost tailor-made for the Californian sun. For many years the Alfas supplied to American customers were almost identical to those for the European markets, but then the arrival of exhaust emissions and safety regulations peculiar to the US market resulted in variations in specification.

Today, now that Europe has toughened up its own emissions and safety rules, there are again virtually no differences between a European and an American Spider, but on the way to this standardization there have been considerable variations, both stylistic and mechanical, which makes separate detailing appropriate.

The alterations centre mainly on the engine's breathing system as a response to emissions regulations, to front and rear end styling as a result of the need to provide 5mph-impact bumpers, and to lighting arrangements. The needs of the American marketing department also produced some differences in standard interior equipment and suspension calibration. It is not clear whether American-specification Spiders and GTVs always ran on softer springs and dampers, but they certainly did from the late Sixties (probably around the time they were fitted with 14in rather than 15in wheels) and they came with a very substantial-looking skid-plate below the sump to immunize it from the effects of bottoming.

Since both the Spider and the GTV were on sale at the time the new US rules took effect, both models began to diverge from their European

specification. However, the GTV died in the mid-Seventies, which meant that it escaped some of the unfortunate reshaping that the Spider had to endure. When the first emissions regulations were imposed for 1968 model year cars, Alfa Romeo appeared to be asleep, and the company actually withdrew from the market for a season while it prepared a solution. This turned out to be the replacement of the twin Weber carburettors with fuel injection made by Spica, itself a division of Alfa Romeo.

The Spica injection system was used in US Alfas from 1969 to 1981 and so accounts for a considerable percentage of Alfa's US production run, besides being used in the Montreal, the GTA Junior racers and even in Alfa's flat-12 Formula One engine. But it actually started life as a pump for diesel engines in trucks, and was then adopted for the use of the 1750 105-series models.

The objective of the injection system was to achieve more faithful management of the engine's breathing, tighter fuel metering producing closer control of its exhaust emissions and so a better chance of satisfying the regulations. It was the only chance of doing so, in fact, because the twin Webers were unable to produce the level of accuracy required.

The Spica system used an engine-driven mechanical pump, propelled at half crankshaft speed by a glassfibre belt, and inside it lay a quartet of variable displacement plungers actuated by a miniature crankshaft. The rear half of the pump housed a mechanical logic unit to determine the quantity of fuel injected. It did this by rotating a series of collars around each plunger via a gear rack and a link, whose position was largely established by throttle angle, although ambient temperature and engine speed also played a role.

The plungers were supplied with fuel by a high-speed electric pump, also made by Spica, located at the rear of the car. However, reliability troubles with this pump resulted in it being replaced in 1975 by a Bosch device which was internally cooled by the fuel flow.

Prior to this modification there came another rethink, this one serious enough for the cars once again to be withdrawn from sale (for the 1970 model year) while Alfa carried out more work on the injection system, this time improving it sufficiently for the basic design to survive until 1981. Quite a number of Alfas were sold during the 'missing' 1968 and 1970 seasons, however, the cars entering the United States via Canada thanks to a loophole in the law, so there is no cause to be baffled should one stumble on such an example.

Views on the desirability of cars equipped with the Spica injection equipment are mixed, one school claiming that, properly adjusted and serviced, the system adds to the car's refinement as well as to its performance. The other camp reasons that, first, fuel injection is not part of a traditional Alfa, and second, the system is very difficult to set up and highly unlikely to function reliably. I happen to fall into the second category, having been involved for a while with a 1978 US-specification Spider that seemed to have taken up idleness as a profession. Junking the Spica kit, however, rejuvenated the car remarkably, although the wallet took quite a battering at the time.

As a rule, keeping the car the way it was built probably makes sense if you live in the United States because the spares and expertise will be available. However, in Britain, familiarity with the system is about as rare as the Spica equipment itself (although supplies can be obtained from EB Spares) and the expense of some components probably makes it more economical in the long run to convert to carburettors. Be aware, though, that this is not the straightforward job that it might seem – blanking off the hole in the cylinder block to which the injection pump bolts is just one of many time-consuming tasks on the agenda. The only advantage in sticking with the system in the UK is that later cars came with a catalyst, enabling the Spider to be run on unleaded fuel and with a cleaner conscience.

Apart from this major mechanical change, and the continuation of the Duetto's lower 4.56:1 rear axle ratio (the European models had 4.1:1 units), the 1968 Spider and GTV can be identified by their orange marker lights at the end of each flank, 'iniezione' boot badges and, in the Spider's case, a strange and rather crude strip of chrome covering the grille, presumably a limp attempt to protect it from parking bashes.

The next round of changes came with the 1971 model year cars, their improved fuel injection yielding an extra 3bhp (prompting a Veloce tag) and eliminating flat-spots that marred the original attempt. This also coincided with major changes for all Spiders when the Kamm-tail styling was adopted, along with a mass of other detail changes. There were minor alterations for the GTV, too. But the only other modification to the American part of their specification, apart from the mechanical tweaks already mentioned, was the adoption of larger rectangular side identification lights, which were recessed into the front and rear wings.

As if a two-season absence was insufficient, Alfa managed a third in 1972 when there was a delay in the arrival of the new 2000 Spider and GTV. When they eventually emerged as 1973 model year cars they turned out to be virtually identical to their European counterparts, the only differences being the fuel injection, the marker lights and the addition of seat belt warning lamps. The GTV continued more or less unchanged until its demise in 1974, but the Spider was to live on and change quite noticeably as the American regulations became ever more demanding.

Several changes came in 1975. Apart from the switch to the Bosch electric fuel pump, an air pump was also installed, hung at the front of the engine from a rather crude bracket, and the exhaust manifold, previously four-into-two-into-one, was changed to a more restrictive four-into-one device.

But the biggest change was external, where some substantial new bumpers were hung from each end. They were needed to meet the 5mph crash test stipulating that the car should suffer no damage should it meet with a solid object at this speed. To satisfy it, the bumpers contained hefty steel girders, were wrapped in sizeable slabs of rubber and were bolted to a pair of shock absorbers. They protected the previously rather vulnerable Alfa most effectively, but they had about as much grace as a drunken sumo wrestler. The rear bumper was simply over-sized, and the front one made a real mess of what had previously been some very delicate sculpting in steel and chrome. The Alfa shield was swamped, and the badge was set into the bumper itself, below which some rather crude indicators were hung.

The Spider was to look this way until 1983, when there was another facelift, but there would be more changes under the bonnet as the emissions requirements stiffened. California again led the way, its rules being harder to meet than those of the remaining 49 states, the upshot being that it was the first territory to demand the standard fitment of a catalyst. This arrived with the 1977 model year Spider which, rather surprisingly, offered 8bhp more than the 103bhp 49-state cars, the catalyst having allowed Alfa to fit a freer-flowing manifold to these cars.

This gave them a 0–60mph time of 10sec and a top speed of 104mph, which meant that the cars were fast enough to be fun, although they were far from tarmac shredders. There was little in the way of change for the Spider for the next few seasons, though from 1978 all were supplied with the catalyst that had first been fitted to the Californian models. The 1979 model year changes saw some minor upgrades to the interior, including new door armrests with built-in storage bins, revised shaping for the seats and a flat luggage area behind them.

A technical innovation arrived the following year, though, in the shape of Alfa's variable valve timing device. A very compact assembly attached to the end of the inlet camshaft, it used oil pressure and a centrifugal valve to alter the cam timing. By retarding the intake cam 20 degrees at idle before advancing both it and the spark timing at 1,650rpm, performance, fuel economy and emissions output were all said to have been improved, although Alfa admitted that it could not point to increased peak torque and bhp figures to prove it. Instead, the system simply widened the torque curve, the most noticeable effect for the driver being a gain in low-speed flexibility.

Not that the Spider tested by *Car and Driver* in January 1981 went particularly well, the car recording a 0–60mph time of 12.1sec and a top speed of just 99mph. The magazine put this down to the tightness of the test car, but the main reason was the taller final-drive ratio (4.1:1) which had lengthened the gearing.

Towards the end of 1981, for the 1982 model year, there were some major mechanical changes, the most significant being that the Spica fuel-injection set-up was ditched in favour of a Bosch L-Jetronic system, as fitted to the GTV6. The Bosch system was far more accurate and responsive, dispensing with the need for an air pump and increasing the likelihood of finding someone who knew how to fix it. The ignition was now flywheel-triggered, further improving engine management precision.

The bodywork was also changed again, though not visibly this time, in that it had been further strengthened to reduce scuttle shake. However, personal experience of both pre-and post-1981 model year cars suggests that this was less effective than it might have been – the 1978 car with which I was familiar for a while suffered far less shudder than a brand new 1991 model, despite having covered over 80,000 miles.

Alfa offered two versions of the car for the 1982 model year, the familiar Veloce, which came with electric windows, air conditioning and a variety of other luxury features, and a model known as the Enthusiast's Spider, which did without all the trimmings in return for a lower price. Just 400 of these cheaper cars were built to test the market, presumably with less than encouraging results because the model was dropped the following year.

In any case, 1983 saw the car rejuvenated with the restyled front and rear based on Pininfarina's Aerodinamica exercise, at which point the specifications of American and European Spiders converged. The only significant difference then was the US cars' mandatory catalyst, the remaining variations being down to the question of which markets standardized on such options as air conditioning, alloy wheels, leather trim, power windows, and so on.

However, the American market has been offered a wider range of cars than Europe with the introduction in 1985 of another stripped-out model, this time called The Graduate after the film of that title. Moreover, this time the exercise was successful because the model was still current six years later.

As this is being written, there are no longer any significant differences between American and European Spiders, and their specifications have become even closer now that a catalyst has become a standard fitment in virtually every market. For a while this made later-model Spiders a better prospect for importation from the United States, but now that so many of the more recent cars are available in Europe the economics of shipping them across from the United States has become less attractive. This means that the rubber-bumpered, Spica-injected cars have become the more common imports, not least because they are so cheap to buy in the United States that the cost of importation has become so attractive, superficially at least.

Driving the 2000 GTV

It is a good idea not to expect too much the first time you step into a GTV, at least not if you have just emerged from a decent modern car. It is not that the Alfa is a bad car – in its day it was one of the best, which is why people want them now – but that expectations have moved on and what was pronounced as satisfactory in 1972 may not seem quite so clever today. A period of mental adjustment is needed, and it can take longer than one might think.

But once this process has been completed it is hard not to enjoy a GTV, and for more than mere antique charm because it is still a seriously quick car, has an engine that is the measure of any modern 2-litre, and handles in an enjoyably diverting style. And in addition there is that pleasure of driving a car that is exceptionally stylish and rarely seen.

The most vivid first impression, once you have climbed inside, is the low seating position and the almost unrestricted panorama through the glasshouse, thanks to those slim pillars. Shortly afterwards comes the realization that if the seat is positioned to suit your arms relative to the steering wheel your legs become somewhat bunched, or vice versa. Welcome to Latin cabin architecture, which is designed for those short of leg and long of arm, in other words most of those who live in the leg of Italy.

Unless one fits a wheel even more dished than the one already provided there is little to be done about this, so it is just as well that the seats are exceptionally comfortable. The 2000 GTV was lauded for having among the few orthopaedically satisfactory chairs available in cars in the early Seventies, and they stand comparison even now,

particularly in the shape of the backrest, which is superbly well contoured.

But the GTV scores less well in other ergonomic departments. The indicator stalk is an unbelievably vague affair, switching from dip to main beam is a bit of a fiddle, and the brake and clutch pedals are floor-hinged, making them less than easy to tread. There are worse about, however. The remainder of the switchgear is distributed over an inconveniently wide area, though in right-hand-drive cars your left arm does get used to dropping on to the wiper and blower toggles, which lie just ahead of the handbrake.

For all that, the GTV is scarcely a wrestle to drive – it simply requires more effort than, for example, a Toyota Celica. This is especially true of the steering at a crawl, though once the GTV is rolling the effort at the steering wheel rim lightens considerably to deliver far more feel than the Toyota, or most other modern sports cars for that matter, can provide.

This is one of the most appealing features of the GTV – the delightfully tactile experience of steering it. Loosen your grip a little and let that wood-rimmed wheel, which is such a pleasure to grasp, writhe gently in your palms and you begin to learn that this car is a sensitive tool, one that will reward those who use it well. It is not a car to be thrown about brutally (though both it and its driver will probably survive such treatment), but one in which the pleasures are derived from driving cleanly, steering tidily through turns, braking smoothly to slow the car, and tapping the throttle to neatly match revs and gears.

And what gears! The Alfa's five-speeder sets a standard that was unchallenged for many years because the ratios were easy to find and the lever moved with such oily precision. Today, the stick looks strange, sprouting from the centre console at 45 degrees, and its movements are unnecessarily long, but the feeling that you are actually moving oiled cogs rather than some flimsy rubber-wrapped linkage provides a sensation that is all too rare.

The twin-cam four-cylinder engine provides still more delight. It may be about as easy to rouse as a hung-over drunk on a cold morning, but once fired up and warm it is a terrifically eager engine. Crisp and instant throttle response mark it apart from modern motors, the result of having those twin Webers nuzzling their throats against the cylinder-head to fire fuel straight into the flames. No fuel-injected car can match its reactions, nor the gurgling suck and roar of carbs greedy for air.

The upshot of these fuelling arrangements, apart from making the GTV rather swift (8.9sec for 0–60mph and a flat-out 122mph are possible) is that the engine can be metered very precisely with the accelerator. The slightest depression produces a lower engine note and a surge of motion, the slightest relaxation a noticeable slowing as compression checks the car. This means it is so much easier to match the GTV's pace to the ebb and flow of a twisting, dipping road to produce a fluency of progress that makes driving the car such a joy.

But fluent is not the word to use to describe the Alfa's ride, which is probably the most dated facet of the car. Lofty tyre walls it may have, but that live back axle likes to jig and buck over the rough stuff, rarely settling and never managing much more than merely rounding off the bumps. On poor roads progress is jostling, but the upside is that the GTV is rarely knocked badly off-course because the axle is quite firmly tied down. One can feel this at walking pace, when the back end can be detected performing a curious sideways waddle over bumps as the T-piece does its stuff.

That the axle is so firmly reined in is one reason why the GTV handles so well despite such an apparently archaic arrangement; a live axle was becoming ancient for a car of this calibre even when the GTV was new. Of course, a decently engineered double-wishbone front suspension helps. The car plunges into corners with aplomb, its rear end sinking reassuringly under power and the front end clinging true to allow satisfyingly explosive eruptions from bends on a regular basis.

The same is less true in tight corners, though, when the GTV's inclination to roll can lift the inside rear wheel high enough to spin it a little, a problem that is likely to be short-lived because of the need to back off to curb the understeer that tends to build in hairpins. If the car has a limited-slip differential (as most 2000s do) this is less of a problem, but it is a fact that the Alfa is a bit cumbersome through slow twists.

Rip through a succession of shallower curves, on the other hand, and the car satisfies deeply. This is when the thing balances so well, demanding no more than fractions of lock to trace precise lines of attack, the body poised as it rolls slightly from side to side. There is no understeer here, none of the nose-heaviness that undermines the best of today's GTIs, just the feeling that a change of direction is unforced, that the car never has to fight physics to follow the road. And that is intoxicating.

Stir in that rich, burbling exhaust note, the lemon-sharp throttle response and that creamy gearchange, and you have a recipe for real enjoyment, and never mind the car's weaker nature.

It does have one, though, dynamically as well as ergonomically. Grip, for instance, is less than super-abundant, especially in the wet. In the dry it takes some effort to make the back end step out of line, but on wet tarmac it is all too easy to have the GTV mimicking a crab. You have to be quick with the wheel to catch it, too, because the snap can be quite sudden. However, once you have mastered the technique, wet roundabouts can become a source of high entertainment.

The brakes are good, too, which is a major reassurance. In fact if they are properly set up (which is not always easy with these twin-servo cars) they can prove to be exceptionally effective, and repeatedly so thanks to generously dimensioned discs. They tend to get well used, too, if you make the best of the engine with its abundance of instantly available torque. Those carburettors help, but the fat torque curve is what makes this such an effortless car, and for anyone used to a modern 16-valve machine this potency will come as something of a shock. There is no need to rev this motor, no need to drop a couple of gears to get past drifts of dawdlers – just squeeze the throttle and the GTV surges past. It is effective enough to make one think that maybe the promoters of multi-valve technology have got it all wrong, and maybe they have. With the torque shaped the Alfa's way the engine wears out more slowly, the gearshifting arm has less work to do and the ears take less of a battering.

Not that the Alfa is a particularly quiet car. The engine is vociferous when worked hard, subtly insistent at a cruise, and a burbling friend when just ambling along. The suspension crashes a bit at times and tyre roar is always there, if not as hummingly persistent as in some German cars. But what really undermines the GTV as a relaxing long-distance tourer is wind noise, which gushes from around the front pillars and the quarter-lights. Opening a glass triangle alters the pitch of the roar, but never eliminates it altogether. If the radio is to be heard at 85mph it has to be turned up, loud.

So the GTV cannot be called a soothing car, though it is certainly not wearing. It is just that it has to be consciously driven, unlike most of today's cars which whisk you along so easily that you barely notice the roads. With those you have to do a bit of steering, a bit of braking and a bit of accelerating from time to time, but mostly you just sit there, a third party to progress. In an Alfa it's simply not like that. Put some effort into driving it and you get a rich reward. You're involved, a part of the action, which is what makes these cars so intoxicating and, for so many of us, so completely irresistible.

APPENDIX C

Driving the current Spider

If one is going to be cold-blooded about it, owning today's Alfa Spider is about as sensible as living in a thatched cottage in which the water is supplied from a well and the light is provided by candles. The Spider's innards are as ancient as the British Police's Z-Cars. But these days age seems to be part of the Alfa's appeal – it may be impractical, at times a pain even, but it has an old-world charm that is hard to resist. It has class, too, more than the MX-5, for example, even if Mazda's pretty sportster is unquestionably the better car. And since when did rational judgment play a major role in buying sportscars?

In any case, the Spider does not appear to be outmoded, in fact it looks decidedly modern from some angles, the new nose and tail which Pininfarina gave it in 1989 blending very successfully with the body's unaltered torso. A cursory glance at the cabin suggests recent design, too. But anyone who has driven in an older

Spider will soon rediscover the wrinkles that give its age away.

The dashboard, for example, is basically the same moulding that emerged in 1971, but it houses a modern, glass-fronted instrument binnacle, different air vents and extra padding at its base to protect legs in an accident. The gearlever still sprouts at 45 degrees, but it emerges from a new centre console (these are cheap to tool up) sheathed in leather and plastic, and the driving position is as inconvenient as ever for northern Europeans, though it is not hopelessly uncomfortable.

Loads of details live on unchanged, like the hood clips, the sun-visors, the interior door handles – though these are matt black now – as well as the pedal rubbers, and the seat recline knobs which work in the opposite sense to those of every other car.

But apply the mind and you notice how much things have changed in detail. For a start, there is no longer the ritual of prodding the accelerator repeatedly in order to wet the Weber carburettors' throats, and an end to the delicate business of balancing choke and hand throttle; the suck and gobble of gagging carbs has gone. Move off, though, and there are clear reminders of the past. First gear still crunches if you fail to move the lever into second beforehand, and the fuel gauge needle's engaging habit of waving wildly when the Spider corners or mounts a bump is faithfully preserved, even if the dial looks different. (An undamped needle can be quite useful – if it fails to move from 'empty' as you either corner or brake violently you know for sure that an involuntary halt is imminent.)

Another quirk living on is that characteristic rear end waddle over bumps taken at a crawl – it is the axle's T-shaped locator that causes it. But there is a big surprise from the chassis, which is that grip is way above the levels achieved by the older Spiders. Wider rubber is part of the reason, the remainder being down to modern tyre technology and the modest amount of fettling which the suspension has received over the years.

So the modern Spider has a useful amount of grip in the dry (it is not as sticky in the wet, limited-slip differential or not), but it lacks the handling precision of a modern sportscar. Driving effort is reduced by the power steering, but so is the wonderful feel through the steering wheel rim which used to be such an attraction of these cars. Not that the assistance is badly judged by today's standards, it is just that the steering is not the tactile treat that it used to be.

What the car really lacks is wieldiness. You can't say that it understeers badly (it doesn't oversteer much, either), but it is more cumbersome than a modern GTI, and it becomes agitated by bumps, sometimes needing quite a bit of redirection on the rougher country roads. Concentration is called for.

There is also a lack of precision in some of the controls, the brakes, for example, being over-servoed (the nose really dives towards the ground if you tread hard) and the gearchange surprisingly sticky and resistant. This gearbox always had long throws between the ratios, but it seems as though the leather gaiter and the plastic knob also impede. Perhaps more bedding-in miles would have helped the car which was tested.

And what of the performance? Well, it's there – this car is as quick as an eight-valve Golf GTI – but the engine is a bit reticent about serving up serious 'go'. It doesn't pull sportingly hard until 4,000rpm is seen on the dial, by which time the twin-cam engine is sounding unfamiliarly harsh and reluctant. This is not the engine that Alfa enthusiasts have been used to, though those who have experienced the first of the injected Alfettas will recognize the sensation – sadly, this version of the famous four seems to be the least attractive there has been from the enjoyment angle, even if it is clean and efficient with its variable inlet valve timing and standard three-way catalyst.

So far, then, a litany of drawbacks, yet somehow it is all forgiven. It is not merely the folding hood that compensates, either, because one feels warm towards the car whether or not there is a lid over your head. There is something friendly in its nature, a feeling that you and it are in this together. It's a thought which is reinforced by a long drive because there is a kind of 'battling the elements' feel to long hauls on the motorway as the wind and the engine roar, leaving you to entertain yourself with thoughts because the radio cannot make itself heard.

Then, when you have nearly reached your destination, you just fold back that canvas, amble along in the sunshine and calm down. That is how the Spider is best sampled. Driven gently it requires less effort, there's time to take in the view, and you escape being battered and buffeted by the wind.

Not that efforts have not been made to turn the Spider into something closer to a practical car. In Britain, at least, an interestingly styled glassfibre hardtop is supplied as standard, and it comes with a heated rear window, a headlining and a cabin light which promise to turn the Spider into a snug little coupe for winter. But such promise soon evaporates once this headgear is aboard. It is not that the hardtop leaks or that it doesn't fit properly (though it takes a two-man, 10-minute wrestle to get it firmly installed), but that it makes the car so confoundedly noisy. You hear the whistle and rush of wind even at 35mph – add more speed and you can even imagine you're beneath the canopy of a cloud-racing Spitfire. The din is almost unbearable on a long journey, and really it is preferable to use the hood, which doesn't rattle, causes less wind noise, seats snugly and is still the easiest lid to lower of any production car, including the latest Mercedes-Benz SL, the electric motors of which need an age to wind the roof into its compartment.

The remainder of the Spider's luxury kit is less of a disappointment. The electric windows rise and fall with surprisingly swift authority, the leather-dashed seats look as though they have been hijacked from a Ferrari and details like the courtesy light delay and the ribbed luggage deck behind the seats heighten the idea that this is the kind of car that boutiques would sell if only they had the space.

There are a few little irritations, though. The boot and fuel filler releases are not transferred if the car is a right-hand-drive conversion, the steering wheel boss looks cheap, and the wires that enliven the hardtop look desperately crude sprouting from beneath the carpet at the rear. They provide a clue to the build standards throughout the car, which is not assembled with Nineties-style precision. Nor does it enjoy today's usual level of corrosion protection. For example, there is little evidence of wax injection, the paint thickness seems inconsistent and such underseal as appeared on the car tested seemed to have been applied somewhat lazily. For the buyer of a new Spider, job number one should be to get out the Waxoyl and douse every cave, crevice, corner and orifice within the body, otherwise a restoration job may well be underway sooner than one might expect.

But despite all this it is impossible not to like the Spider. It manages to be an acceptable extravagance, somehow, a car not so ostentatious that it offends, yet is different enough to win admiring glances. It is not a precision driver's tool, but there is pleasure to be had from punting it along a winding road, sufficient 'go' in it to keep ahead of most of the tin-box shoal. Best of all, perhaps, it is a romantic nostalgia trip that can be bought new, and there are few enough of those around these days.

Alfa Romeo's 1974 range, clockwise from the Alfasud 1.2 TI, the 2000 Berlina, Alfetta 1.8 saloon, Giulia Super, Spider, Montreal V8, GT Junior, Alfasud and Alfetta GT, the replacement for the 105-series GTV. The Alfetta GT was styled by Giugiaro, as its predecessor had been, and featured a rear-mounted gearbox for improved traction and handling balance, though a terrible gearchange was also the result. Note the evidence of the Alfa habit of keeping on old models after production of their successors has begun. ALFA ROMEO ARCHIVES

APPENDIX D

Model identification and reference data

MODEL DESIGNATIONS

Note: Alfa Romeo's naming policy seems designed to create maximum disarray for those who are involved with these cars, although some sense can be made of it with familiarity.
Reference to the first part of the chassis number is a help, this being why, for example, post-1959 Giuliettas are sometimes referred to by the more dedicated enthusiast as 101-series cars. The following is a guide to these numbers, the first three digits of which refer to the generic family of cars and the second two to the model type within the series.

Chassis code	Model	Period made
101 SERIES		
101 12	Sprint Normale	1962–64
101.18	Spider Veloce	1964–65
101.21	Sprint Speciale	1963–65
101.23	Spider Normale	1962–65
101.23	4R Zagato	1965
105 SERIES		
105.02	Sprint GT	1963–66
105.03	Duetto	1966–67
105.08	4R Zagato	1966–67
105.11	TZ	1963–67
105.11	TZ 2	1965–67
105.12	Berlina 2000	1971–78
105.14	Ti Berlina	1962–67
105.16	Ti Super	1963–64
105.21	2000 GTV	1971–76
105.24	Spider 2000	1971 to date
105.25	GTC	1964–66
105.26	Super Berlina	1965
105.30	1300 GT Junior	1968–72
105.32	GTA	1965–67
105.36	1600 GTV	1965–68
105.39	1300 Ti Berlina	1966–72
105.44	1750 GTV	1967–72
105.48	1750 Berlina	1967–72
105.51	1750 GTV USA	1968–72
105.57	1750 Spider	1967–71
105.59	1300 GTA Junior	1968–72
105.62	1750 Spider USA	1968–72
105.64	Montreal	1971–77
105.71	1750 Berlina USA	1968–72
105.91	1300 Spider Junior	1968–72
105.93	1300 Junior Z	1970–72
115 SERIES		
115.00	2000 Berlina USA	1971–74
115.01	2000 GTV USA	1971–74
115.02	2000 Spider USA	1971–74
115.07	1600 Junior (110bhp)	1972–75
115.24	1600 Junior Z	1972–75
115.35	1600 Junior (102bhp)	1974–81
115.38	2000 Spider (128bhp)	1975–82
115.35	1.6 (102bhp) Aero	1983–86
115.38	2.0 (128bhp) Aero	1982–86
115.60	2.0 (128bhp) Aero QV	1985–89
115.62	1.6 (104bhp) Aero	1986–89
115.66	2.0 (128bhp) Aero	1986–89
115.A1	2.0 (126bhp) S4	1989 to date
115.A2	1.6 (109bhp) S4	1989 to date

SPECIFICATIONS

Note: Where possible, both DIN and SAE power and torque figures are provided, the DIN figures, which are in almost universal use today, being shown first. SAE figures are higher because they are taken when the engine is relieved of the need to drive most of the ancillary equipment.

Consequently, they are less realistic, but SAE was the most popular measure during the life of the Giulietta and the early days of the Giulia Sprint and Spider.

ALFA ROMEO GIULIETTA SPRINT 1300 1954–62, reintroduced 1964–65

ENGINE
Configuration: In-line, four-cylinder. Construction: Aluminium alloy cylinder block, cast-iron liners, five main bearings, aluminium alloy cylinder head with hemispherical combustion chambers and centrally placed spark plugs. Dimensions: Bore and stroke 74mm x 75mm, capacity 1,290cc. Compression ratio 8.0:1 to late-1958, 8.5:1 thereafter. Valve gear: Twin overhead camshafts, two valves per cylinder angled at 80deg, valve diameters 31mm inlet, 28mm exhaust, exhaust valves sodium-filled, duplex timing chain. Fuel system: Mechanical fuel pump, single dual-choke Solex 32 PAIAT carburettor, 11.6gal/53l fuel tank. Ignition: 12V battery, coil, distributor, 14mm spark plugs. Lubrication: Pressurized by gear-driven pump, full-flow filter. Cooling: Water-cooled via centrifugal pump, belt-driven fan and radiator. Max power: 65bhp (SAE) at 6,100rpm, 80bhp (SAE) at 6,300rpm from late-1958. Max torque: 79.5lb/ft at 4,000rpm to late-1958.
TRANSMISSION
Type: Four-speed manual, all-synchromesh except reverse. Ratios up to March 1964: 1st 3.258, 2nd 1.985, 3rd 1.357. 4th 1.000, reverse 3.252:1; after March 1964: 1st 3.304, 2nd 1.988, 3rd 1.355, 4th 1.000, reverse 3.010:1. Final drive ratio 4.555:1. Rear axle: Rigid with light-alloy differential casing, hypoid-bevel final drive.
CHASSIS AND BODY
Construction: All-steel, monocoque. Front suspension: Independent by coil springs and double wishbones, anti-roll bar, telescopic shock absorbers. Rear suspension: Live axle with trailing arms, coil springs, locating A-arm hinged to body and differential casing through rubber bushes, telescopic shock absorbers. Steering: Worm and roller, 2.8 turns lock to lock. Wheels: 4.5J x 15in. Tyres: 155-15in. Brakes: All-drum, disc front from March 1964. Mechanical handbrake acting on rear drums.
DIMENSIONS
Wheelbase 93.7in/2,380mm; front track 50.9in/1,292mm; rear track 50.0in/1,270in; overall length 156.5in/3,975mm; overall width 60.5in/1,537mm; overall height 52.0in/1,321mm; kerb weight 1,938lb/880kg.
PERFORMANCE
Max speed (80bhp model) 103mph, 0–60mph 13.2sec (Road & Track).

ALFA ROMEO GIULIETTA SPRINT VELOCE 1956–62

As for Sprint 1300 except:

ENGINE
Compression ratio 9.1:1. Fuel system: Twin horizontal dual-barrel Weber 40 DCO3 carburettors. Max power: 90bhp (SAE) at 6,500rpm. Max torque: 86.8lb/ft at 4,500rpm.
TRANSMISSION
Final drive ratio 4.1:1.
DIMENSIONS
Kerb weight 1,973lb/895kg.
PERFORMANCE
Max speed 112mph, 0–60mph 12.1sec (Factory).

ALFA ROMEO GIULIETTA SPIDER 1300 1955–62

As for Sprint 1300 except:

DIMENSIONS
Wheelbase 86.7in/2,200mm, 88.6in/2,250mm from 1959; overall length 152.0in/3,861mm, 153.9in/3,909mm from 1959; overall width 61.0in/1,549mm; overall height 51.0in/1,295mm; kerb weight 1,896lb/860kg.
PERFORMANCE
Max speed (65bhp model) 100mph, 0–60mph 14.8sec (Road & Track).

ALFA ROMEO GIULIETTA SPIDER 1300 VELOCE 1956–62

As for Sprint 1300 except:

ENGINE
Compression ratio 9.1:1. Fuel system: Twin horizontal dual-barrel Weber 40 DCO3 carburettors. Max power: 90bhp (SAE) at 6,500rpm. Max torque: 86.8lb/ft at 4,500rpm.
TRANSMISSION
Final drive ratio 4.1:1.
DIMENSIONS
Wheelbase 86.7in/2,200mm, 88.6in/2,250mm from 1959; overall length 152.0in/3,861mm, 153.9in/3,909mm from 1959; overall width 61.0in/1,549mm; overall height 51.0in/1,295mm; kerb weight 1,905lb/865kg.

ALFA ROMEO GIULIA SPRINT 1600 1962–64

As for Giulietta Sprint 1300 except:

ENGINE
Dimensions: Bore and stroke 78mm x 82mm, capacity 1,570cc. Compression ratio 9.1:1. Valve gear: Valve diameters 35mm inlet, 31mm

exhaust. Fuel system: Single twin-choke Weber carburettor. Max power: 92bhp (SAE) at 6,200rpm.

TRANSMISSION
Type: Five-speed manual, all-synchromesh except reverse. Ratios: 1st 3.304, 2nd 1.988, 3rd 1.355, 4th 1.000, 5th 0.791, reverse 3.010:1/ Final drive ratio 5.125:1

CHASSIS AND BODY
Brakes: disc front, drum rear.

DIMENSIONS
Kerb weight 1,993lb/905kg.

PERFORMANCE
Max speed 107mph (Factory).

ALFA ROMEO GIULIA SPIDER 1600 1962–65

As for Sprint 1600 except:

DIMENSIONS
Wheelbase 88.6in/2,250mm; overall length 153.9in/3,909mm; overall width 61.0in/1,549mm; overall height 51.0in/1,295mm; kerb weight 1,949lb/885kg

PERFORMANCE
Max speed 106.5mph, 0–60mph 12.5sec (*Cars Illustrated*).

ALFA ROMEO GIULIA 1600 SPIDER VELOCE 1964–65

As for Spider 1600 except:

ENGINE
Compression ratio 9.7:1. Fuel system: Twin horizontal dual-barrel Weber 40 DCOE carburettors. Max power: 112bhp (129bhp SAE) at 6,500rpm. Max torque: 96lb/ft at 4,500rpm.

TRANSMISSION
Final drive ratio 4.555:1.

PERFORMANCE
Max speed 109mph, 0–60mph 10.5sec (*Road & Track*).

GIULIETTA AND GIULIA 1600 PRODUCTION VOLUMES

Giulietta Sprint	24,084
Giulietta Sprint Veloce	3,058
Giulietta Spider	14,300
Giulietta Spider Veloce	2,796
Giulia 1600 Sprint	7,107
Giulia 1600 Spider	9,250
Giulia Spider Veloce	1,091
TOTAL	61,686

ALFA ROMEO GIULIA SPRINT GT 1963–66

ENGINE
Configuration: In-line, four-cylinder. Construction: Aluminium-alloy cylinder block, cast-iron liners, five main bearings, aluminium-alloy cylinder head with hemispherical combustion chambers and centrally placed spark plugs. Dimensions: Bore and stroke 78mm x 82mm, capacity 1,570cc. Compression ratio 9.0:1. Valve gear: Twin overhead camshafts, two valves per cylinder inclined at 80deg, valve diameters 35mm inlet, 31mm exhaust, exhaust valves sodium-filled, duplex timing chain. Fuel system: Mechanical fuel pump, twin horizontal dual-barrel Weber 40 DCOE 4 carburettors, 10.1gal/46l fuel tank. Ignition: 12V battery, coil and distributor, 14mm spark plugs. Lubrication: Pressurized by gear-driven pump, full-flow oil filter. Cooling: Water-cooled via centrifugal pump, belt-driven fan and radiator. Max power: 106bhp, (122bhp SAE) at 6,000rpm. Max torque: 103lb/ft at 3,000rpm.

TRANSMISSION
Type: Five-speed manual, all-synchromesh except reverse. Ratios: 1st 3.304, 2nd 1.988, 3rd 1.355, 4th 1.000, 5th 0.791, reverse 3.010:1. Final drive ratio 4.555:1. Rear axle: Rigid with light-alloy differential casing, hypoid-bevel final drive.

CHASSIS AND BODY
Construction: All-steel, monocoque. Front suspension: Independent by double wishbones and coil springs, anti-roll bar, telescopic shock absorbers. Rear suspension: Live axle with trailing arms, coil springs, locating T-arm hinged to the body and differential casing through rubber bushes, telescopic shock absorbers. Steering: Recirculating ball or worm and roller, 3.25 turns lock to lock. Wheels: 4.5J x 15in perforated steel. Tyres: 155-15in. Brakes: All-disc, diameters 11.25in/286mm front, 9.75in/248mm rear. Mechanical handbrake acting on shoes located within drums machined into rear hubs.

DIMENSIONS
Wheelbase 92.5in/2,350mm; front track 51.5in/1,310mm; rear track 50.1in/1,270mm; overall length 160.5in/4,080mm; overall width excluding mirrors 62.2in/1,580mm; overall height 51.7in/1,315mm; kerb weight 2,090lb/950kg.

PERFORMANCE
Max speed 112mph, 0–60mph 10.6sec (*Road & Track*).

ALFA ROMEO GIULIA GTC CABRIOLET 1964–66

As for 1600 GT.

ALFA ROMEO GIULIA SPRINT GT VELOCE 1965–68

As for Sprint GT except:

ENGINE
Valve gear: Valve diameters 37mm inlet, 31mm exhaust. Fuel system: Twin horizontal dual-barrel Weber 40 DCOE 27 carburettors. Max power: 109bhp (125bhp SAE) at 6,000rpm. Max torque: 103lb/ft (115lb/ft SAE) at 2,800rpm.
CHASSIS AND BODY
Steering: 3.8 turns lock to lock. Tyres: 155SR-15in. Brakes: Disc diameter 10.7in/272mm front, 10.5in/267mm rear.
DIMENSIONS
Kerb weight 2,244lb/1,102kg.
PERFORMANCE
Max speed 112mph, 0–60mph 10.5sec (*Road & Track*).

ALFA ROMEO 1300 GT JUNIOR 1968–74

As for 1600 GT except:

ENGINE
Dimensions: Bore and stroke 74mm x 75mm, capacity 1,290cc. Valve gear: Valve diameters 33mm inlet, 28mm exhaust. Fuel system: Twin horizontal dual-barrel Weber 40 DCOE 28 carburettors. Max power: 89bhp (103bhp SAE) at 6,000rpm. Max torque: 101lb/ft (SAE) at 3,200rpm.
TRANSMISSION
Ratios: 5th 0.86:1.
CHASSIS AND BODY
Steering: 3.6 turns lock to lock. Tyres: 155SR-15in. Brakes: Disc diameter 10.7in/272mm front, 10.5in/267mm rear, servo added end-1967.
DIMENSIONS
Kerb weight 2,046lb/930kg.
PERFORMANCE
Max speed 102mph, 0–60mph 13.8sec (*Motor*).

ALFA ROMEO 1750 GTV 1967–72

As for 1600 GT except:

ENGINE
Dimensions: Bore and stroke 80mm x 88.5mm, capacity 1,779cc. Compression ratio 9.5:1 on early cars, later 9.0:1. Valve gear: Valve diameters 38mm inlet, 31mm exhaust. Fuel system: Twin horizontal dual-barrel Weber 40 DCOE 32 carburettors. Max power: 122bhp at 5,500rpm on 9.5:1 CR, 118bhp (135bhp SAE) at 5,500rpm on 9.0:1 CR. Max torque: 137.4lb/ft at 2,900rpm.

TRANSMISSION
Final drive ratio 4.1:1.
CHASSIS AND BODY
Rear suspension: Anti-roll bar added. Steering: 3.8 turns lock to lock. Wheels: 5.5J x 14in perforated steel. Tyres: 165HR-14in. Brakes: Disc diameters 10.7in/272mm front, 10.5in/267mm rear, dual circuits after 1970, servo, twin servoes on RHD cars.
DIMENSIONS
Front track 52.1in/1,324mm; rear track 50.1in/1,274mm; overall length 161.4in/4,100rpm, kerb weight 2,292lb/1,040kg.
PERFORMANCE
Max speed 115.5mph, 0–60mph 9.3sec (*Motor*).

ALFA ROMEO 2000 GTV 1971–76

As for 1600 GT except:

ENGINE
Dimensions: Bore and stroke 84mm x 88.5mm, capacity 1,962cc. Valve gear: Valve diameters 38mm inlet, 31mm exhaust. Fuel system: Twin horizontal dual-barrel Weber 40 DCOE or Solex C40 DDH-5 or Dellorto DHLA 40 carburettors, 11.7gal/53l fuel tank. Max power: 132bhp (150bhp SAE) at 5,500rpm. Max torque: 134lb/ft (152.6lb/ft SAE) at 3,000rpm.
TRANSMISSION
Final drive ratio 4.1:1. Optional mechanical limited-slip differential.
CHASSIS AND BODY
Rear suspension: Anti-roll bar added. Steering: 3.8 turns lock to lock. Wheels: 5.5J x 14in perforated steel, optional spoked alloy. Tyres: 165HR-14in. Brakes: Disc diameters 10.7in/272mm front, 10.5in/267mm rear, dual circuits, servo, twin servoes for RHD cars.
DIMENSIONS
Front track 52.1in/1,324mm; rear track 50.1in/1,274mm; overall length 161.4in/4,100mm; kerb weight 2,288lb/1,040kg.
PERFORMANCE
Max speed 115.3mph, 0–60mph 8.9sec (*Motor*).

ALFA ROMEO 1300 GT JUNIOR 1974–76

As for 1600 GT except:

ENGINE
Dimensions: Bore and stroke 74mm x 75mm, capacity 1,290cc. Valve gear: Valve diameters 33mm inlet, 28mm exhaust. Fuel system: Twin horizontal dual-barrel Weber 40 DCOE 28 carburettors. Max power: 89bhp (103bhp SAE) at 6,000rpm. Max torque: 101lb/ft (SAE) at 3,200rpm.

CHASSIS AND BODY
Rear suspension: Anti-roll bar added. Steering: 3.6 turns lock to lock. Tyres: 155HR-15in, 165HR-14in optional. Brakes: Disc diameters 10.7in/272mm front, 10.5in/267mm rear, dual circuits, servo, twin servoes for RHD cars.
DIMENSIONS
Front track 52.1in/1,324mm; rear track 50.1in/1,274mm; kerb weight 2,250lb/1,020kg.

ALFA ROMEO GIULIA 1600 GT JUNIOR 1972–76

As for 1600 GT except:

ENGINE
Valve gear: Valve diameter 37mm inlet. Fuel system: Twin horizontal dual-barrel Weber 40 DCOE carburettors. Max power: 110bhp (125bhp SAE) at 6,000rpm; from 1974 102bhp (116bhp SAE). Maximum torque: 115lb/ft (SAE) at 2,800rpm; from 1974 119lb/ft (SAE) at 2,900rpm.
CHASSIS AND BODY
Rear suspension: Anti-roll bar added. Steering: 3.6 turns lock to lock. Wheels: 5.5J x 15in perforated steel, optional 5.5J x 14in. Tyres: 155HR-15in, optional 165HR-14in. Brakes: disc diameters 10.7in/272mm front, 10.5in/267mm rear, dual circuit, servo, twin servoes for RHD cars.
DIMENSIONS
Front track 52.1in/1,324mm; rear track 50.1in/1,270mm; kerb weight 2,244lb/1,020kg.
PERFORMANCE
Max speed 112mph, 0–60mph 10.3sec (*Sports Car World* – Australia).

ALFA ROMEO GIULIA GTA 1600 1965–69

ENGINE
Configuration: In-line, four-cylinder. Construction: Aluminium alloy cylinder block, cast-iron liners, five main bearings, aluminium alloy cylinder head with hemispherical combustion chambers and twin-spark plugs. Dimensions: Bore and stroke 78mm x 82mm, capacity 1,570cc. Compression ratio 9.7:1 (10.5:1 race spec). Valve gear: Twin overhead camshafts, two valves per cylinder inclined at 80deg, valve diameters 40.5mm (36mm race spec) inlet, 36.5mm (30mm race spec) exhaust, exhaust valves sodium-filled, duplex timing chain. Fuel system: Mechanical fuel pump, twin horizontal dual-barrel Weber 45 DCOE 14 carburettors (plus modified air intake for race spec), 10.1gal/46l fuel tank, 19.8gal/90l optional. Ignition: 12V battery, twin coils, twin distributors, eight 14mm spark plugs. Lubrication: Pressurized by gear-driven pump, full-flow oil filter (oil cooler for race spec). Cooling: Water-cooled via centrifugal pump, belt-driven fan and radiator. Max power: 115bhp (133bhp SAE) at 6,000rpm, (170bhp at 7,500rpm race spec). Max torque: 119lb/ft (148lb/ft race spec) at 5,500rpm.
TRANSMISSION
Type: Five-speed manual, all-synchromesh except reverse. Ratios: 1st 3.304, 2nd 1.988, 3rd 1.355, 4th 1.000, 5th 0.791 (0.850 race spec), reverse 3.010:1. Final drive ratio 4.555:1. Rear axle: Rigid with light-alloy differential casing, hypoid-bevel final drive, mechanical limited-slip differential.
CHASSIS AND BODY
Construction: Monocoque, steel floor and core structure, aluminium external body panels. Front suspension: Independent with double wishbones and coil springs, anti-roll bar, telescopic shock absorbers. Rear suspension: Live axle, trailing arms, coil springs, sliding block, telescopic shock absorbers (revised roll centre and anti-roll bar for race spec). Steering: Recirculating ball or worm and roller. Wheels: 4.5J x 15in light alloy. Tyres: 155HR-15in (5.50L-14 race spec). Brakes: All-disc. Mechanical handbrake acting on shoes located within drums machined into rear hubs.
DIMENSIONS
Wheelbase 92.5in/2,350mm; front track 51.5in/1,310mm; rear track 50.1in/1,270mm; overall length 160.5in/4,080mm; overall width 62.2in/1,580mm excluding mirrors; overall height 51.6in/1,310mm; kerb weight 1,641lb/745kg.
PERFORMANCE
Max speed over 115mph (135.7mph race spec), 0–62mph figure not available for standard car (7.6sec race spec) (Factory, *Ruoteclassiche*).

ALFA ROMEO GIULIA GTA 1300 JUNIOR 1968-71

As for GTA 1600 except:

ENGINE
Dimensions: Bore and stroke 78mm x 67.5mm, capacity 1,290cc. Compression ratio 9.0:1. Max power: 96bhp (110bhp SAE) at 6,000rpm; race spec 160bhp at 7,800rpm with carburettors, 165bhp at 8,400rpm with Spica fuel injection.
TRANSMISSION
Ratios: 1st 2.540, 2nd 1.700, 3rd 1.260, 4th 1.000, 5th 0.790:1. Final drive ratio 4.555:1 (race spec).
CHASSIS AND BODY
Tyres: 165HR-14in. Dimensions: Front track 52.1in/1,324mm; rear track 50.1in/1,270mm; overall height 51.7in/1,315mm; kerb weight 1,674lb/760kg.
PERFORMANCE
Max speed 109mph (130.5mph race spec) (Factory)

ALFA ROMEO GIULIA GTA-SA SOVRALIMENTATO 1967–68

As for GTA 1600 except:

ENGINE
Dimensions: Bore and stroke 86mm x 67.5mm, capacity 1,570cc. Compression ratio 10.5:1. Fuel system: Twin horizontal dual-barrel carburettors, twin pump-driven centrifugal superchargers, 19.8gal/90l fuel tank. Max power: 220bhp (250bhp SAE) at 7,500rpm.
CHASSIS AND BODY
Tyres: 550M-14in.
DIMENSIONS
Front track 52.1in/1,324mm; rear track 50.1in/1,274mm; overall length 155.9in/3,960mm; overall height 52.0in/1,320mm; kerb weight 1,718lb/780kg.
PERFORMANCE
Max speed 149mph (Factory).

ALFA ROMEO 1750 GT Am and 2000 GT Am 1970–71

As for 1600 GTA except:

ENGINE
Dimensions: Bore and stroke 84.5mm x 88.5mm, capacity 1,985cc. Compression ratio 11.1:1. Valve gear: Valves inclined at 45deg. Fuel system: Twin electric fuel pumps, Spica indirect fuel injection, 21.9gal/100l fuel tank. Max power: 195–220bhp (SAE) at 7,200rpm (1970), 210–240bhp (SAE) at 7,500rpm (1971).
CHASSIS AND BODY
Tyres: 9–13in.
DIMENSIONS
Front track 54.5in/1,385mm; rear track 53.5in/1,360mm; overall width 65.7in/1,668mm; overall height 52.0in/1,320mm; kerb weight 2,026lb/920kg (1970), 2,070lb/940kg (1971).
PERFORMANCE
Max speed 137mph (1970), 149mph (1971) (Factory).

GIULIA SPRINT GT AND GTV 1963–75
PRODUCTION VOLUMES

Giulia Sprint GT	21,850
Giulia Sprint GTC	1,000
Giulia Sprint GT Veloce	12,499
Giulia GTA 1600	493
GT 1300 Junior	91,964
GTA 1300 Junior	492
1750 GTV	44,276
2000 GTV	37,921
TOTAL	210,495

ALFA ROMEO 1600 SPIDER DUETTO 1966–67

ENGINE
Configuration: In-line, four-cylinder. Construction: Aluminium alloy cylinder block, cast-iron liners, five main bearings, aluminium cylinder head with hemispherical combustion chambers and centrally placed spark plugs. Dimensions: Bore and stroke 78mm x 82mm, capacity 1,570cc. Compression ratio 9.0:1. Valve gear: Twin overhead camshafts, two valves per cylinder inclined at 80deg, duplex timing chain. Fuel system: Mechanical fuel pump, twin horizontal dual-barrel Weber 40 DCOE 27 carburettors, 10.1gal/46l fuel tank. Ignition: 12V battery, coil distributor, 14mm spark plugs. Lubrication: Pressurized by gear-driven pump, full-flow oil filter. Cooling: Water-cooled via centrifugal pump, belt-driven fan and radiator. Max power: 109bhp (125bhp SAE) at 6,000rpm. Max torque: 103lb/ft (115lb/ft SAE) at 2,800rpm.
TRANSMISSION
Type: Five-speed manual, all-synchromesh except reverse. Ratios: 1st 3.304, 2nd 1.988, 3rd 1.355, 4th 1.000, 5th 0.791:1. Final drive ratio 4.555:1. Rear axle: Rigid with light-alloy differential casing, hypoid-bevel final drive.
CHASSIS AND BODY
Construction: All-steel, monocoque. Front suspension: Independent by double wishbones and coil springs, anti-roll bar, telescopic shock absorbers. Rear suspension: Live axle with trailing arms, coil springs, locating T-arm hinged to body and differential casing through rubber bushes, telescopic shock absorbers. Steering: Recirculating ball or worm and roller, 3.75 turns lock to lock. Wheels: 4.5J x 15in perforated steel. Tyres: 155-15in. Brakes: All-disc, diameters 11.25in/286mm front, 9.75in/248mm rear. Mechanical handbrake acting on shoes located within drums machined into rear hubs.
DIMENSIONS
Wheelbase 88.6in/2,250mm; front track 51.6in/1,310mm; rear track 50.0in/1,270mm; overall length 167.3in/4,250mm; overall width 64.2in/1,630mm; overall height 50.8in/1,290mm; kerb weight 2,181lb/990kg.
PERFORMANCE
Max speed 111mph, 0–60mph 11.2sec (*Motor*).

ALFA ROMEO 1750 VELOCE 1967–71

As for 1600 Duetto except:

ENGINE
Dimensions: Bore and stroke 80mm x 88.5mm, capacity 1,779cc. Compression ratio 9.5:1, later 9.0:1. Valve gear: Inlet valve diameter 37mm. Fuel system: Twin horizontal dual-barrel Weber

40 DCOE carburettors. Max power: 122bhp (132bhp SAE) at 5,500rpm with 9.5:1 CR, 118bhp at 5,500rpm with 9.0:1 CR. Max torque: 127lb/ft (137.4lb/ft SAE) at 2,900rpm.

TRANSMISSION
Final drive ratio 4.1:1.

CHASSIS AND BODY
Rear suspension: Anti-roll bar added. Wheels: 5.5J x 14in. Tyres: 165HR-14in. Brakes: All-disc, diameters 10.7in/272mm front, 10.5in/267mm rear, dual circuits after 1970, servo, twin servoes for RHD cars.

DIMENSIONS
Front track 52.1in/1,324mm; rear track 50.1in/1,274mm; overall length after 1970 162.2in/4,120mm; kerb weight 2,292lb/1,040kg.

PERFORMANCE
Max speed 116.4mph, 0–60mph 9.2sec (*Motor*).

ALFA ROMEO 2000 VELOCE 1971–82

As for 1600 Duetto except:

ENGINE
Dimensions: Bore and stroke 84mm x 88.5mm, capacity 1,962cc. Valve gear: Inlet valve diameter 38mm. Fuel system: Twin horizontal dual-barrel Weber 40 DCOE, Solex C 40 DDH-5 or Dell'Orto DHLA 40 carburettors, 11.2gal/51l fuel tank. Max power: 132bhp (150bhp SAE) at 5,500rpm, 128bhp at 5,300rpm after 1975. Max torque: 134lb/ft (152.6lb/ft SAE) at 3,000rpm, 132lb/ft at 4,300rpm after 1975.

TRANSMISSION
Final-drive ratio 4.1:1. Optional mechanical limited-slip differential.

CHASSIS AND BODY
Rear suspension: Anti-roll bar added. Wheels: 5.5J x 14in perforated steel, optional spoked alloy. Tyres: 165HR-14in. Brakes: All-disc, diameters 10.7in/272mm front, 10.5in/267mm rear, dual circuits, servo, twin servoes for RHD cars.

DIMENSIONS
Front track 52.1in/1,324mm; rear track 50.1in/1,247mm; overall length 162.2in/4,120mm; kerb weight 2,291lb/1,040kg.

PERFORMANCE
Max speed 116mph, 0–60mph 8.8sec (*Autocar*).

ALFA ROMEO 1300 JUNIOR 1968–78

As for 1600 Duetto except:

ENGINE
Dimensions: Bore and stroke 74mm x 75mm, capacity 1,290cc. Valve gear: Valve diameters 33mm inlet, 28mm exhaust. Fuel system: Twin horizontal dual-barrel Weber 40 DCOE 28

carburettors. Max power: 89bhp (103bhp SAE) at 6,000rpm. Max torque: 101lb/ft (SAE) at 3,200rpm.

TRANSMISSION
Ratios: 5th 0.860:1.

CHASSIS AND BODY
Wheels: 4.5J x 15in perforated steel, 14in optional after November 1970. Tyres: 155-15in, 165SR-14 optional after November 1970.

DIMENSIONS
Front track 52.1in/1,324mm; rear track 50.1in/1,274mm; overall length after November 1970 162.2in/4,120mm; kerb weight 2,181lb/990kg.

PERFORMANCE
Max speed 106mph (Factory).

ALFA ROMEO 1600 JUNIOR 1972–75

As for Duetto except:

ENGINE
Max power 110bhp at 6,000rpm, 102bhp at 6,000rpm after 1974. Max torque 103lb/ft at 2,800rpm, 105lb/ft at 2,900rpm after 1974. Fuel system: Twin downdraught dual-barrel Dellorto DHLA 40 or Solex C40 DDH6 carburettors.

CHASSIS AND BODY
Wheels: 4.5J x 15in perforated steel, optional 4.5J x 14in. Tyres: 155HR-15in, 165HR-14in optional.

DIMENSIONS
Front track 52.1in/1,324mm; rear track 50.1in/1,274mm; overall length 162.2in/4,120mm; kerb weight 2,247lb/1,020kg.

PERFORMANCE
Max speed 115mph (Factory).

ALFA ROMEO SPIDER 2.0 AERODINAMICA 1982–89

As for 2000 Veloce (rather than 1600 Duetto) except:

ENGINE
Fuel system: Twin horizontal dual-barrel Solex C40 ADDHE carburettors. Max power: 128bhp at 5,300rpm. Max torque 132lb/ft at 4,300rpm.

CHASSIS AND BODY
Tyres: 185/70HR-14in.

DIMENSIONS
Overall length 168.1in/4,270mm; kerb weight 2,291lb/1,040kg.

PERFORMANCE
Max speed 118mph, 0–62mph 9.0sec (Factory).

ALFA ROMEO SPIDER 2.0 (fuel injection and catalyst) 1986–89

As for Spider 2.0 above except:

ENGINE
Fuel system: Bosch L-Jetronic injection with three-way catalyst. Max power: 115bhp at 5,500rpm. Max torque: 119lb/ft at 3,000rpm.
DIMENSIONS
Kerb weight 2,357lb/1,070kg.
PERFORMANCE
Max speed 115mph.

ALFA ROMEO SPIDER 1.6 1983–89

As for 1600 Junior except:

ENGINE
Fuel system: Twin horizontal dual-barrel Weber 40 DCOE carburettors. Max power: 104bhp at 5,500rpm, 5,900rpm after 1986. Max torque: 105lb/ft at 2,900rpm, 101lb/ft at 4,300rpm after 1986.
CHASSIS AND BODY
Wheels: 5.5J x 14in. Tyres: 165R-14in.
DIMENSIONS
Overall length 168.1in/4,270mm; kerb weight 2,247lb/1,020kg.
PERFORMANCE
Max speed 112mph (Factory).

ALFA ROMEO SPIDER 2.0 SERIES FOUR 1989 to date

As for 2000 Veloce except:

ENGINE
Compression ratio 10.0:1. Valve gear: Variable intake valve timing device. Fuel system: Electric fuel pump, Bosch Motronic ML4.1 ignition and injection system, plus optional three-way catalyst. Cooling: Thermostatically controlled electric fan.

Max power: 126bhp (120bhp with catalyst) at 5,800rpm. Max torque: 124lb/ft (116lb/ft with catalyst) at 4,200rpm.
TRANSMISSION
Optional ZF three-speed automatic.
CHASSIS AND BODY
Steering: Power-assisted, column adjustable for height and rake. Wheels: 6J x 15in aluminium alloy. Tyres: 195/60R-15in.
DIMENSIONS
Overall length 167.6in/4,258mm; kerb weight 2,445lb/1,110kg.
PERFORMANCE
Max speed 118mph, 0–62mph 9.0sec, 9.4sec with catalyst (Factory).

ALFA ROMEO SPIDER 1.6 SERIES FOUR 1989 to date

As for 1600 Junior except:

ENGINE
Fuel system: Twin horizontal dual-barrel Weber carburettors. Ignition: Electronic breakerless. Cooling: Thermostatically controlled electric fan. Max power: 109bhp at 6,000rpm. Max torque: 101lb/ft at 4,800rpm.
CHASSIS AND BODY
Steering: Power-assisted, column adjustable for rake and height. Wheels: 5.5J x 14in perforated steel. Tyres: 185/70R-14in.
DIMENSIONS
Overall length 167.6in/4,258mm; kerb weight 2,357lb/1,070kg.
PERFORMANCE
Max speed 112mph, 0–62mph 10.0sec (Factory).

SPIDER 1966–91 PRODUCTION VOLUMES

1300	7,237
1600	19,474
1750	8,701
2000	83,396
TOTAL	118,808